Cocoa at Midnight

Kathleen Clifford was born in a West London slum in 1909. Her family lived from hand to mouth in rented rooms near Paddington Station. At school she dreamed of working in Whiteley's, a glamorous department store, but instead she worked in service. After she retired from service Kathleen returned to Paddington – and got that job in Whiteley's! Kathleen Clifford died in 1989.

Tom Quinn is the editor of *Country Landowner's Magazine*. He has written several books for small independent publishers. He has spent the past twenty years interviewing people who worked in domestic service, getting them to tell him their life stories.

Also in the Lives of Servants series:

The Maid's Tale – Rose Plummer with Tom Quinn
The Cook's Tale – Nancy Jackman with Tom Quinn
They Also Serve – Bob Sharpe with Tom Quinn

Cocoa at Midnight

Kathleen Clifford
written with Tom Quinn

CORONET

First published in Great Britain in 2013 by Coronet
An imprint of Hodder & Stoughton
An Hachette UK company

First published in paperback in 2013

1

A CIP catalogue record for this title is available from the British Library

ISBN 978 1 444 73595 6

Typeset by Hewer Text UK Ltd, Edinburgh
Printed and bound by CPI Group (UK) Ltd, Croydon, CR0 4YY

Hodder & Stoughton policy is to use papers that are natural, renewable
and recyclable products and made from wood grown in sustainable
forests. The logging and manufacturing processes are expected to
conform to the environmental regulations of the country of origin.

Hodder & Stoughton Ltd
338 Euston Road
London NW1 3BH

www.hodder.co.uk

Chapter 1

She was far too big for the pram but we pushed her in it anyway. Nora Pittance she was called. Her head lolled about and she dribbled but we liked that because we could clean her up and pretend she was a *real* baby. Shocking looking back, but her mum and dad were glad to have her out of the house and she never knew who or where she was. Everyone said she had water on the brain and was spastic.

She must have been three years old and she was blonde and pretty except for the rolling eyes and the dribble. We pushed her round the streets like a doll, only she was alive. I hope to God that we weren't horrible to poor Nora and I hope she looked out of that pram and at least enjoyed the sunshine. My best friend Elsie Greenway and I loved playing this game and I think Elsie really wanted to make Nora happy because Elsie herself had something to worry about. She was clever I think and I thought she was pretty, but she had a big strawberry birthmark on her face. She used to say, 'Give me a kiss, Kate. You can keep yer eyes closed!'

All our play was in the streets. I don't think we ever went to a park because parks seemed really empty to us. All that green grass and far fewer people than were on the street.

If we didn't have Nora we'd push an empty pram and talk like our mothers and argue about how much washing and shopping we had to do. I can remember repeating the things my mother said with the greatest seriousness. Play without toys was always about pretending to be grown-up, which is mad when you think being grown-up back then was just a world of toil and trouble. But children never understand these things.

Elsie and I were as close as sisters until we lost touch, seemingly for ever, after she went to one junior school and I went to another.

But in those happy days of playing in the street I'm afraid we were not always as good as we should have been. We did a bit of thieving because we were desperate for sweets. Elsie and I would leave Nora outside and go in the local shop where Elsie would immediately start talking to the shopkeeper in a very rapid manner and with the most confident air you can imagine:

'Hello, Mrs Short, how are you today? We're fine thank you for asking and for the time of year. We thought we'd come in and have a talk with you because you look lonely and it might bring some luck and some customers. We also want to look at the sweets as we'll have some money next week . . .'

And on she'd go, with Mrs Short, the shopkeeper, folding her arms and looking increasingly fed up and angry or amused depending on her mood. Eventually when Elsie looked as if she might just run out of steam, Mrs Short would interrupt and say:

'Elsie, you say that every time you come in here and then while you're at it your friend there pinches a sherbet or two and you think I don't see.

'I'll give you a sherbet today so you don't have to steal but mind you pay me back when you can.'

'Yes, Mrs Short,' said Elsie and out she'd troop.

'She really likes us, doesn't she?' said Elsie as we split the sherbet between us.

But if Paddington in the 1920s was bad for ordinary poor kids then it was bloody murder for kids with disabilities. Nora died before she was six and at the time I thought nothing of it. People were always dying but I think of her often now and hope she can forgive me.

Chapter 2

People say that women had to fight for the right to work, but when they say that they mean middle-class women. All those delicate lace-covered girls you see in Victorian pictures fanning themselves on the chaise longue and looking like their arms would snap if they didn't have someone to hold their tea cups for them. Working-class women like me have always worked. I reckon we worked much harder even than the working-class men who swaggered around the place. Certainly they worked long and often back-breaking hours but when they got home in the evening that was it. They stopped. Down came the braces off their shoulders and out came the packet of fags, feet up by the fire and 'Where's me dinner, missus?'

It wasn't so good for their wives. Having slaved all day making matches in a factory or taking in washing or looking after six kids they then slaved at the cleaning and cooking in the evenings and sometimes half the night.

Of course not everyone worked hard. A lot of men got their money on a Friday and spent it in the pub that night and clouted their wives if there was a word of complaint. The poor wives were down the pawnshop every Monday with anything they could find.

We knew a young couple who were both always drunk and whose kids were always on the street, until they vanished for good, one by one – street Arabs we used to call kids like that. Their mum and dad were drunk twenty-three hours out of four and the kids were out at all times and took up with anyone. You never saw them after they reached the age of about ten or twelve because they'd hopped it permanently by then.

But I'm getting ahead of myself.

Chapter 3

I was born in Paddington in West London in 1911. According to my mother, a slightly tipsy midwife dropped me out of the towel two minutes after I'd arrived.

'She even had the cheek to swear when she dropped you,' my mum used to say. 'Didn't even apologise, just scooped you up and said, "She's all right, ain't even dusty."'

Paddington was all horse dung and railway smoke. You could smell both most days, especially in summer, and it was a real laugh to watch the boys run out as soon as a horse did his business in the road because you could make a bit of money, maybe a ha'penny a bag, out of manure. There was a lot of it in the streets but the middle classes were happy to pay the kids to scoop it up for them.

We used to go into the shunting yards at Paddington to look at the horses. The station kept its own massive cart horses to move goods around the yard and sometimes to move the engines. My dad had a job for a while mucking them out but he wasn't a country boy and said he found them terrifying because they were unpredictable.

'There's a big black one,' he told me, 'and he keeps his white eye on you. Soon as you're between him and the wall of his box the bastard moves across and just leans on you. Hardly seems to shift more than an inch from one foot to the other but he's so bloody big you can't breathe a bit. It's a ton and a half of horse meat leaning on your lungs. But he doesn't want to kill you. Oh no. He just does it long enough to show you who's boss. And when he's not leaning on you the bastard's always trying to stand on yer feet!'

My dad was a terrible one for exaggerating and he always made out every job was so awful that much as he'd been prepared to stick it, he'd been forced to give it up. It wasn't that he was a lazy old bugger – well, he was in some ways – it was always that no sane person could stick a job like that. But despite the fact that he never stayed in a job for five minutes he always had money. Not a lot but enough.

'As long as you've got a jingle in your pocket you're all right,' he used to say twenty times a day. And then he'd jingle the change in his pocket, smile and bounce off down the stairs. He never once told my mother where he was going. Men never told their wives let alone their children. It was a pride thing. The woman was supposed to do for her husband and children and it was not for her to question what her old man got up to. Some men would clout their wives for even asking and men who helped their wives or stayed at home with them were laughed at by their friends and soon didn't have any. And it's a fact that in the 1920s and 1930s up to the Second World War if not beyond, no man in Paddington would ever have been seen pushing a pram – he'd never hear the last of it from his mates.

A time traveller going back to Paddington would notice one thing above all others. The dirt. If the smoke from the trains and the dung from the horses wasn't enough, there was the greasy stale smell of people who didn't change their clothes for weeks and months at a time.

But Paddington was all right in other ways. Every morning I woke to the sounds of the trains' shrill whistles and the distant roar of the steam as they headed up the incline out of the station. There was plenty of work too and Paddington, for all its slums, was close to areas where the quality lived. It was also a bit of a bohemian area and artists and prostitutes were always shouting at the buses or each other or killing themselves.

Years later I read that a painter called Nina Hamnett jumped out of her window in Paddington and fell forty feet onto the railing below, but she was only the most famous. All sorts of people killed themselves in Paddington, but you had to be artistic for anyone to notice.

Not a week went by without a suicide. It was partly because there was no social-security safety net, I think, and when people got desperate they often felt they really did have no other option. Back then suicide was a serious crime and if you survived you were locked up, which always seemed a bit mad to me. It was a nasty, tough old world in lots of ways and ordinary people liked to pretend they were as tough as the world they inhabited. When something bad happened we just gossiped about it. We loved a bit of scandal. We were like the mob that would have gone to a hanging – which always struck me as funny as we lived just a mile or so from Tyburn, now Marble Arch, where all the hangings had taken place centuries earlier. I bet my ancestors were always in the front row.

But imagine it. If you were a woman and you had no husband and no family or if you had kids and your husband had left you, there was no money – which meant you either went on the game or you topped yourself. You had to have your wits about you the whole time because you see there was often nowhere to turn if you were really stuck.

Chapter 4

We had a little flat above a shop in Praed Street a hundred yards from the station. My earliest memory is being given a small wooden doll by my dad. He'd made it himself because he didn't have the money to buy me a doll, but what was really good about it was that he'd not only made the doll. He'd also made it a little dress and hat and shoes as well. Imagine that. Not my mum but my big old tough dad! By the time I'd grown up he was still chuckling about that doll. He said, 'When I gave you that doll I had to tell you not to mention it to anyone in case any of the blokes found out I'd made the clothes. I'd have never heard the last of it!'

Dad was an odd-job man who could turn his hand to anything – he'd even been a screever for a bit. That's a pavement artist.

'I could have gone to the bloody Slade if I'd had the bunce,' he used to say. 'That bloody Augustus John. He can't draw at all. I expect he's heard about me.' That was a good joke because in fact he'd been useless at the pavement drawing and told me he hadn't made a penny.

'I thought it would be easy,' he said, 'money for old rope, but for some reason they didn't like my work. Too modern I suppose. I was always ahead of my time!'

Dad was often in a bad mood, usually when he was out of funds, but every now and then he'd brighten up and be very entertaining. He'd talk nonsense, but it was very entertaining for us kids. Other times the black mood would come down and he'd scowl around the house. Then suddenly he'd be joking about everything again. He had a tatty brown hat he always wore with his dark grey shabby suit, a shirt with no collar – he hated collars – and terrible teeth, crooked, half of them missing and the ones that were left had a terrible green tinge. You'd run a mile if he tried to kiss you. But he had loads of hair that had gone grey early. He was always running his hands through his hair and as his fingers were always covered in tobacco stains his hair took on a permanent orange-brown tint. I never knew what he looked like in old age because he'd long vanished by then.

He used to pretend to be a waiter sometimes when we had our dinner and he'd swank around the table with a dirty old cloth over his arm bowing to each of us kids and saying, 'And what does Her Ladyship require? I can do you a very nice French tongue pie with a crotchety sauce.'

My mum was completely different. Whereas Dad hopped from one job to another, she did the same work the whole of her life. She used to wash and mend for people. Well, that's what she said she did – in fact I only ever saw her washing, but I think she thought mending made the job sound a bit more genteel.

She'd get the washing in and take it to the local baths. You could swim there but they also had rows of baths where people who didn't have a bath at home could go. They had a massive laundry where all the local women would wash their own and other people's clothes. All the big Victorian baths were like that. That's why they were called public baths and wash houses. The swimming pools weren't the most important things about them.

Even in the 1960s the old ladies of Paddington and North Kensington still took their washing down to the wash house at the baths because it was a lot more fun than doing it at home on your own. By then some of these old biddies had spent twenty or thirty years meeting each other once or twice a week and wouldn't miss it for anything. None of them could swim and they rarely had a bath – all they were interested in was the wash house.

But I loved the swimming pool. There was a first-class pool and a second-class pool – the difference was that the posh pool was more expensive and didn't have fag ends floating in it. In the second-class pool they also used to chuck you out after an hour which the kids hated. You'd end up with kids shouting at the attendant, 'Oi mister, I ain't been in ten minutes. That was me bruvver you saw.'

And the attendants would get really angry and shout and swear till the kids climbed out. Once I saw the attendant dive in to get at one particularly annoying kid who promptly hopped out and ran off right out of the building still in his swimming shorts. And I remember his swimming shorts were woollen and half hanging off him. But we cheered him!

When they demolished the old wash houses it was heartbreaking for the old ladies because that's where they'd always met their friends.

I used to go with Mum sometimes when I was six or seven and if she didn't send me in for a swim in the second-class pool, she'd leave me in a funny little room away from the pools and the wash house where the walls were covered with glazed tiles and there were a few benches and marble tables bolted to the floor. There was a wooden hatch in the wall. If you knocked on the hatch it would open and you'd ask for a penny slab and they'd give you a lovely piece of bread pudding for one old penny. I remember the weight of that bread pudding and it was so sweet to me who didn't get shop sweets much. In fact, as is so often the way with all the smells and sounds of childhood, I've never since tasted anything as good as that slab. But I'm sure if I'd gone back as an adult and tried that bread pudding again it would not have tasted as it once did. That's just the way things are.

I think the cleanliness and order of the baths made a great impression on me and gave me a taste for sorting things out. I was such a tidy little thing – which is perhaps why I eventually ended up as a housekeeper running other people's houses. Just such a pity I never really got the chance to run my own.

Anyway they had loads of hot water down at the baths and for a few pennies you could do a ton of washing there. That's where my mum used to go to do the washing she took in. It was back-breaking work and you've never seen anything like the state of her hands. Red raw they were, always. She also had what I thought of as the Paddington look – big beefy arms with the sleeves always rolled up and a ragged apron that covered her from her neck to her knees. She never seemed to take it off. Despite all her hard work she was also amazingly stout without seeming to be fat; she was hard, too, like a barrel, with a permanently cross look on her face and hair that she permed herself using old wire curlers and cigarette papers.

She would sit up late by the coal fire, I remember, with her bare feet in a tin basin of warm water to ease her corns and a fag hanging out of her mouth. She would do her hair blind – or nearly blind. What I mean is that she put the curlers in using a tiny broken mirror – it was about two inches square – and as each curler went in she'd take a squint to see it was just where she wanted it. Why she went through this rigmarole once a week every week when she washed her hair I'll never know because she looked a right bloody fright before and afterwards.

What made it even odder was that most of the time as she went about the street or down to her work at the baths she kept the curlers in so you rarely got to see her hair in its lovely wavy state anyway.

Our neighbour Mrs Ellis used to come round every few weeks and they would cut each other's hair while gossiping about everyone else round about.

My dad used to go to the barber's every two weeks and he always had his eyebrows singed. It was his one little vanity and we always knew when he had it done because he'd come back to the house smelling like he was on fire. It's a mystery why anyone had their hair singed back then because by the 1970s no one had it done. Dad used to say 'It's a gentleman's prerogative,' but going to the barber was for him what the baths were to my mum. He liked to chat to the other men there.

His other great hobby was standing on corners with his mates. If it hadn't been for the lack of money when he didn't have any work, I think he would have been happy to stand around talking to his friends all day every day of his life if only it had left him with a jingle in his pocket.

And talking of haircuts and hairdos reminds me of the biggest upset of my childhood. It came when, aged about eight, I had my hair cut by my mother and it was sold to a wigmaker. We got a few bob for it, but I was upset for days not so much because I'd lost my hair but because I didn't get the bloomin' money!

But we weren't poor at all compared to some. There were always people who were so badly off they made the rest of us seem like millionaires. The Irish were the worst. Bloody hell, they were poor! I got friendly with an Irish family that lived along the street from us because they had a daughter my age. The first time I went to call for her there were about six of them in one room with a metal trunk and a couple of chairs the only furniture I could see. But her family were lovely to me, always welcoming. I don't think one of them could read or write a word and the children never went to school at all like the rest of us. The oddest thing of all was that every now and then they would talk to each other in a language that was strange to me. I couldn't understand a word of it. They were speaking Irish of course. As soon as I arrived they would speak in English. That's the curious thing I remember most about them. They had nothing but they had better manners than most of the people I worked for later on.

Chapter 5

At home we always had enough to eat, but I can't believe how stupid we were about food. Meat was always boiled or fried or roasted, cabbage and other vegetables were boiled to mush and salt and pepper were the only seasoning we ever used. No wonder English cooking had such a bad name – in truth there was no cooking involved at all. It was all boil and burn. When I learned to cook later on I was amazed at how the middle classes ate far better food. They always looked to France in cooking matters, though not of course in matters of morality – 'she's a bit French' was a slang way of saying that someone was promiscuous.

Anyone going back to those early days in Paddington would be shocked at the state of the flat where we lived: dark varnished floorboards, a few old beds, a creaky table and chairs and a cooker. That was it. Nothing on the walls and the landlord would have died rather than part with a penny to paint the walls. They'd been whitewashed in about 1900 I'd say and were yellow with coal smoke. The ceiling too was yellowed and bowed and cracked with age.

The house was also overrun with mice and an occasional rat. We bought penny traps that were devils for catching your fingers but as fast as we caught them new mice came in.

But the rats were the worst. You knew when the house had rats because they'd eat almost anything and you'd hear them and see the remains of anything they ate which might include bits of rubber, straw and even plaster. Mice are pickier and you'd rarely see evidence of what they'd been eating. You'd just see a quick darting movement across the room early one morning.

Catching the rats was a horrible business. They were so crafty the only way you could do it was to get some birdlime and paint it thickly on to a wooden board and leave the board where you knew the rats ran along the skirting. A rat would come along at night and his feet would get stuck on the boards. Terrible thing to hear a rat screaming but they did until my dad got along to them and bashed them with a wooden club he kept by the bedhead for burglars. I had nightmares for years in which all I heard was the scream of a rat caught in the birdlime.

Chapter 6

I woke up one morning when I was about eight and I couldn't move – not a muscle. I had no pain but couldn't lift my arms or move my legs an inch. I had to shout for my mother.

They got the penny doctor in and he said it was polio. My poor mother sat down and rested her head on her hands. My father stared at the doctor as if he wanted to hit him. When the doctor had gone there were no specialists to call in. Ordinary people had to deal with disaster on their own in those days.

Mum and Dad came over to the bed and I remember they just stood and stared down at me, struck dumb by the disaster. I tried again and again to move my legs and arms, but nothing happened. I don't recall feeling upset or panic-stricken as you'd think I might. I was calm and almost enjoyed the sense that I could now stay in bed as long as I liked.

'How do you feel, Kat?' said my mother.

'I'm all right,' I said, more to reassure her than anything else. 'I just can't move right now but I'm sure I'll be up and about again soon. I don't feel sick at all.'

The truth is I was intrigued by this new state of affairs. Kids don't seem to panic in these sorts of circumstances, I think. They can't imagine that things might really be terrible unless they are in pain or feel abandoned.

I stayed in bed all that day and the next. Then something strange started to happen. It started when I thought to myself, Hang on, I can't go to the loo in bed, I'm too old. I imagined the shame and boy did I need to go by now. I felt horribly stiff but somehow, almost I think through force of will, I got the engine going again a bit. I found I could move a little again. I had pins and needles everywhere for a while, but I managed to get to the loo to the amazement of Mum.

Truth is I don't think that bloody doctor knew a thing. I can't really have had polio because I never heard of anyone getting paralysed with polio and then recovering. So it was a mystery and it remained a mystery forever after. My mum and dad were just grateful I was up and about again and the horror of what to do with a paralysed girl had passed. But that was just the sort of thing that gave doctors a bad name. People never remembered when they did some good, but they never forgot when a doctor made a bad diagnosis.

What's the point of the doctor? people would say. Bloody charlatans. They give you coloured water and charge you ten bob for it. And of course a lot of them did give you coloured water because it was all so unregulated and unscientific then, you see.

I only ever had one real clue about what might have happened. In the 1950s I had to have a chest X-ray and the doctor told me it was a miracle I was alive because there was a lot of scarring on my lungs. I'd had TB as a girl he told me, and he said it was a miracle it had not spread and killed me. He said he'd never seen anything like it.

Chapter 7

A bigger shock came when I was about ten and I woke up one morning to find my little brother was dead in bed – he'd have been about two years old. He'd been the pet of the family and we couldn't get over the shock for months. That was a dark time and no jokes even from my dad as we moped through the days and weeks as you would expect. After a quick visit by the police to check we didn't look like the sort who would murder someone, we got the undertaker and Natty went into the ground. No pathologist's report or coroner's inquest that I can remember. Too many kids died of all sorts of things for there to be too much of a fuss. It was a very strange death too.

When I'd woken up that morning Natty had had his fingers curled round one of my much bigger fingers and he just looked as if he was asleep. I remember staring at his cute little face as I gradually woke up and started to think about the day ahead. It was only when I went to tickle him to wake him up that I felt how cold he was. I knew he shouldn't have been cold because the bed was so warm.

I remember how we all sat in the miserable morning light staring at the little still boy on the bed while my mother walked up and down with an old handkerchief pressed to her face and absolutely silent. Then she started to wring her hands. I always thought that it was a bit of a cliché about people wringing their hands but they really do it – or at least my mother did. The desperation of that movement always seemed worse to me even than the tears.

Then the neighbours came in and sat around which was an odd sort of comfort and what people always did then. Births and deaths – that's what brought people together. Death and grief were more public then and the need to make the visitors tea while they looked on gave a curious other-worldly feel to an otherwise disastrous day. Half the street came in and out as the day wore on. It was as if they came in shifts.

Chapter 8

So that left four of us. I went to school when I was five. My brother Jack went a year before me and Tom was a good bit older so he'd already left and was wandering the streets and doing odd jobs with my dad. Noel was the baby.

I was very good at figures – arithmetic and algebra I mean. From as early as I can remember I could just see instantly how all the numbers and symbols connected together. They were like a pattern in my head that always made sense without me needing to think much about how to move them around.

I've always felt that my love of numbers and number patterns was connected to the fact that from the earliest I needed to keep things tidy and organised. I mean my few clothes, a pencil or two, even a few pine cones I collected in the park. They had to be in their place neat and tidy always. My dad was amazed when he met one of our teachers and the teacher said, 'You should get Kat into the senior school if you can because she has a good brain – a great flair for numbers.'

My dad was delighted and was always saying to my mum and anyone else who would listen: 'I might be an idiot but my daughter's a genius.' But I know he worried about finding the money for secondary school, which was expensive at that time.

'You don't want to be doing washing, like me,' said my mother. 'You're a good-looking girl with a brain and could get a good job in a nice house with your wages and all your meals – bed and board.'

Mum was convinced that being good at figures would help me get on. She didn't know the first thing about it really but in the long run she was proved right because I would probably have stayed at the bottom of the servant ladder except for the fact that I was such a wiz with numbers – and so tidy and well ordered. Being a housekeeper back then was all about being organised and able to add up!

Chapter 9

But I aspired to more glamorous things in my early days. I thought being a shop girl would be as good as being in the films. And the most glamorous shop in the world was just round the corner from us. Whiteley's in Bayswater was the first and the biggest department store in the world. It was famous at the time. All the girls dreamed of working there and I might really have been able to do it if I could just get a bit more education and learn to speak posh. Mind you there were disadvantages to working at Whiteley's. You had to obey nearly 200 ultra-strict rules, for example, and they gave you the book before you started work. The rules were about dress and behaviour and one slip and you were out.

My friend Ginny laughed when I told her I wanted to work in Whiteley's.

'Yer bloody mad, Kat. What do you want with all those stuck-up tarts? They're not even allowed to have a piss during working hours. Imagine standing there all day with yer legs crossed!'

Ginny was exaggerating but she had a point. For example the Whiteley's rule book said you had to wear long white gloves at all times. If your gloves did not extend at least seven inches above the wrist you would be ticked off. If your stocking seams were not straight two days in a row it was an official warning. You had to work from seven in the morning till eleven at night and live in company accommodation. When I found all this out my dream of shop work faded a bit I must say!

On the other hand I don't think they would have taken me whatever happened with secondary school because you needed to speak properly – not in a strong London accent like me – and a London accent was a hard thing to lose. I was amazed when I discovered that some people really didn't use the word 'ain't'! The other difficulty was that you needed the money for nice shop clothes.

In service, by contrast, you got a uniform and no one cared how you spoke because you weren't allowed to speak! The trouble with service was you had to start at the bottom as a maid and work your way up, which is what I did. By the time I was a housekeeper in a big house I had the sort of life my mum would have loved. Nice and respectable, as she used to say.

For working-class kids in those days real education began when you started work. If you could adapt – adapt the way you spoke and behaved – you would be likely to get on. If you stayed sounding like a local ragamuffin you would never get on.

But for good or ill I went to the senior school while my friends left the juniors and started work. One or two of the girls had boyfriends by then and you knew that come sixteen they'd get married and have to live with their in-laws in some terrible damp basement and then, when the kids started coming, it would all go round again and I didn't want that.

My dad found the money somehow for secondary school because I think that for a while around that time he was doing well on the money front, although I have a horrible feeling his improved finances had something to do with the fact that he'd been up to no good. I say that because he had been summoned to appear in court for something. It was serious because it was referred by the magistrate to the county court or the high court, I don't know which, where it was eventually dismissed for lack of evidence. But he was lucky to get off and he knew it and I think that was his last attempt at anything more than what you might call petty crime.

It took almost a year for all this to take its course and all that time I went to secondary school on the proceeds of his dodgy deals.

When he wasn't trying to be a big-time crook or doing various odd jobs, Dad used to get together with his friends and come up with plans – tip-top schemes he always called them – for making money. They'd go off to Kensington Square or Holland Park where the wealthy lived and, with two of them carrying a ladder, the third would knock on doors trying to persuade people their roofs needed a bit of work or the gutters were leaking. If someone showed the least bit of interest they'd offer just to check and absolutely no charge. Then they'd come down and say the gutter was in a terrible state whether it was or not. My dad said, 'You'd be amazed how many people fall for this.' Oddly, he didn't think there was anything wrong with what he was doing. All his life he'd dodged around for money and anyone who seemed to be well off was fair game as far as he was concerned. But there was some honour among thieves. He'd rather have died than steal from anyone in our little patch of Paddington. 'The toffs won't miss ten shillings,' he'd say, 'and how'd they get their money anyway, that's what I want to know. Do you think they got it honestly? Of course they didn't – it's every man for himself out there, hog eat hog or get eaten by dog.' That's another thing about my dad: whenever he used a phrase like that he always got it slightly wrong. But he was convinced the rich were all robbers and no better than he was. 'The penny-pinching buggers cheat us from morning till night so they can't be surprised when we cheat them back.' He was quite the soap-box man was my dad.

But he never mentioned the thing that got him into court. It was only later that my mum told me what she thought had happened: 'He was shifting stolen stuff between houses in an old handcart. Some of it was good stuff from houses up Kensington way, silver cutlery and that kind of thing. It was bound to lead to trouble.'

What she meant was that the police wouldn't have bothered much if Dad and his mates had been stealing from the poor in Paddington or Notting Dale but as they'd been stealing from the rich, well that was a different matter. The roof was likely to come in.

'Luckily for your dad they picked him up when the cart was empty so they had no real evidence,' said Mum. But going to court scared him a bit and he never tried anything like it again. He even gave up the broken-gutter business and went back to hauling sacks for the stables or getting odd jobs at the station.

But at least Dad's dodgy behaviour meant I got my extra year at school in the senior class with the shopkeepers' sons and daughters. After that year Mum told me I'd have to give it up as it was too expensive and in all truth I'd had enough by then. I felt I was hanging around a bit because it was work for me either sooner or later so it might as well be sooner. I was well into my fifteenth year by the time I got the old heave-ho and I thought of myself as very grownup and mighty sophisticated I can tell you.

I remember the first day after school finished for me was nothing special. I just helped Mum at home, but I was excited deep down because I felt I was grown-up now, which was something I wanted to be more than anything.

Chapter 10

I'd worked a bit on Saturdays in the past, mostly helping my mum or collecting bottles for the returns. You got a ha'penny back for every empty drink bottle returned to the shop in those days because all the bottles were reused and glass was expensive. You knew when you bought the bottle that it was a halfpenny dearer than it would otherwise have been. It was supposed to make you take care of the bottle and not throw it away, but some people did throw them away which is where Ginny and I came in.

We would get an old pushchair on a Saturday morning every now and then and wheel it around the streets looking for bottles that had been left in bins or at the side of the street. It was a right bloody slog but we might make sixpence each at the end of the day after handing the bottles in to a shop.

Only one shop would take the bottles – the others round about hated taking them because they hadn't sold them in the first place and they knew we hadn't bought them. Why that bothered them so much I don't know, but it did. Only Cackles would take them but there were reasons we didn't like going to Cackles.

He ran a small store down a side street that seemed to be filled with the sort of lumber and rubbish that no one could ever possibly sell. There were bags full of old rags, there were stuffed animals and birds, many of them moth-eaten and falling apart, there were rusty old animal traps and lamps and pulleys and wheels and great coils of rope. All along the walls were rusty tins of every size covering the endless shelves that ran up to the ceiling.

Cackles himself was an ugly customer. He must have been about sixty and he had one of those thin faces where the cheeks look as if they have permanently caved in. He was always covered in stubble and long whiskers grew out of his nose which we found fascinating. His thin white hair seemed full of electricity because it stuck up at all sorts of crazy angles. He always wore tartan trousers, a black waistcoat and a filthy white shirt with no collar. He was called Cackles because he had a strange, wheezy, croaky way of laughing and he laughed pretty much after everything he said.

We used to discuss going to his shop with our bottles.

'Shall we try somewhere else this time?' I'd ask Ginny.

'No point,' she'd say. 'No one else will pay. Don't worry, I'll let him do me this time.'

That was the embarrassing thing about Cackles. He only paid us for the bottles if we let him touch us.

We hadn't a clue why he wanted to do it and at the time I never thought much of it – old men had disgusting habits whoever they were and you just had to put up with it. And besides he didn't always do it.

So in we would go and Cackles would say the same thing he always said.

'And who have we here, I wonder?' He knew full well who we were but he always said that.

'Don't tell me it's about bottles,' he'd say. 'No more bottles!' Then you would hear the horrible high-pitched laugh from which he got his nickname.

'Go on, get out of it,' he'd growl, turning his back and waving us out of the shop.

'Give us just a ha'penny for two,' Ginny would say.

'How many yer got?' asked Cackles.

'About thirty-five,' I'd say.

He'd pause a minute then and change the subject.

'You're growing all the time aren't you? Always growing.' Then he'd sidle over and say, 'Very well-grown girls.'

While he looked down at the bottles in our little cart he'd be patting us on the head and then he'd run his hand down our backs – sometimes it was me, sometimes Ginny. He'd sort of squeeze your bottom for a while and start breathing heavily. We knew there was something weird about it all, but it never went any further and at least he paid up.

He might ask one of us to sit on his lap for a moment and then finally he'd hand over the dirtiest little handful of coins you can imagine. The odd thing was that he always had coins worn almost away to nothing, coppers from the beginning of Victoria's reign. And he would always give us far less than a ha'penny for each bottle. But we didn't mind – even threepence each was enough for a feast of sweets.

Chapter 11

But collecting bottles wasn't enough. A week or so after leaving school I got a job through a friend for a few shillings a week taking two six-year-old boys to school every day and then collecting them in the evening. Those boys were just like the rest of us except their mum and dad ran a shop, made good money and treated them like royalty. But they were nice little boys and we got on well. They wore little blue sailor suits and were constantly tugging at their over-tight collars – and oh, how they suffered in the summer in their little ties and hats. Like all children they loved stories so I'd make something up as we went along.

'Tell us about the ghost horse,' they'd say.

This was a story about a white horse that local people every now and then claimed to have seen early in the morning galloping through a thick fog, and God knows we had enough thick fogs. I'd make up all sorts of extra details – such as the horse had a man on its back and the man had no head. They loved that.

The boys went to a little private school near Paddington Basin on the canal where the big houses were. I used to take them in the morning and bring them back at night and I remember once waiting by the gate while the children milled around in the schoolyard all looking very miserable. Then I found out why.

The headmaster sprang through a narrow door at the top of a short steep flight of steps on the far side of the yard and immediately started bellowing at the children as he walked up and down swishing a cane and making an angry speech that lasted about ten minutes. He wore a straw hat and a long gown and kept saying, 'Jesus is watching, always watching. How can you hold your heads up when Jesus is watching?' and at that all the children looked at the ground. Then without a word he stalked back into the school and the children walked out through the gate into the road to be carted off by their carers or parents. I asked Maurice, one of my little boys, if this happened every day.

'Not every day,' he said, 'but usually Mondays.' And he was right. For the next few weeks Mondays and Wednesdays were preaching days – sometimes the headmaster would bring a box and stand on it before haranguing the children. Other times he would stride up and down swishing his cane, although I never saw him use it on the children. I always thought he made religion seem a ridiculous thing. I'd never been interested much in it but that headmaster confirmed my view that it was probably all nonsense.

Then almost as suddenly as it had begun my first job came to an end. I was told I was no longer needed for the children. I mooched about a bit for a week or two helping Mum with the laundry business and then I thought: 'I'm not bloody going on like this.'

I was ambitious, you see. I wanted to get out of Paddington not because I particularly disliked it but because I was restless. I wanted to see a bit of the world even if it was only up the road. I told my mum and dad I was going to get myself a job and that was it.

Next day I got up early, looked in the back of the paper my dad used to read and found an address at the back of a servant agency in Mayfair. I got dressed in my best clothes – including the bomb-proof serge knickers we all wore then – and off I went.

I long ago forgot the name of the agency because that was the one and only time I went to one. I've never been so looked down on in my life as I was by the old battleaxe in those dingy backstreet rooms.

Chapter 12

I sat for what seemed like an age in a dingy brown room with a dozen other nervous-looking girls. The walls were painted chocolate brown and through the one dirty windowpane I could see nothing except a line of shabby washing.

At last I was called into another dingy room where I was ushered to a wooden chair. The woman who had waved me in then disappeared and once again I sat waiting. Ten minutes later a woman in a big black hat came in and sat down opposite me on the far side of a massive dark table piled high with papers. She sat sideways, looking out through another small dirty window, not looking at me at all. She reached across the table and helped herself to a few papers seemingly at random. She shuffled in her seat as if she was being bitten by fleas and then said:

'Where do you live?'

I said, 'Paddington, ma'am.'

I'd been told to say ma'am by my dad, but hadn't a clue what it meant. I thought it was a posh way of saying 'mum', but why would I call someone I didn't know 'mum'?

The woman in the black hat shuffled her bottom and then shuffled her papers. She dipped a pen in a big glass inkwell and stirred it about vigorously. Still she hadn't looked at me. She waited and then wrote something down. The pen dripped ink but she didn't seem to notice.

At last she looked up.

'We can perhaps offer you a position as kitchen maid,' she said and handed me a piece of paper which had the following words written on it: 'Wellington House, Hyde Park Corner, Saturday at nine in the morning. Under no circumstances be late.'

And that was the beginning of my future. I sat amazed, staring at the paper, waiting for further instructions, until she said, 'Good day to you.'

I had no idea then that for every servant position they filled the agency received a fee, but for a lowly maid with no experience the fee would not have been much. I heard from butlers and cooks later on that they were often almost grovelled to by agency staff because placing a butler or cook could be very lucrative, but clearly no one ever felt the need to be polite to a fifteen-year-old girl.

My dislike of agencies was not based solely on my own experience.

It was said that agencies sent people down to remote parts of the country to go about the villages offering the parents of poor girls good positions in

London for their daughters. The girls were then brought up to London and kept together in rows of terrible beds in the agencies' attics until positions could be found for them. Then the agency got its fee. The more innocent the girls the better the agency, and future employers liked it. Country girls were always more in demand than city girls like me. We were thought to be less willing to work hard and more likely to be dishonest. Bloody cheek! I thought. What they really liked was that innocent girls from the country could be abused and exploited and would never complain. If you'd told them that they would be working fifteen hours a day in a big house for a bowl of porridge a day and nothing else they'd have nodded and got on with it.

Chapter 13

I had my piece of paper and was determined to use it. All I knew as I set off home was that I had to stand outside this Mr Wellington's house, but I hadn't a clue exactly where it was. I'd never really been much beyond Church Street market at the top of Praed Street, which was about half a mile from where I lived. I'd never been to North London or south of the river or outside London so I wasn't quite as sophisticated as I perhaps thought I was.

'I will be working for Mr Wellington,' I told my mum. 'I wonder who he is?'

'I dunno,' she said.

It turned out that Mr Wellington was the Duke of Wellington who had been dead almost a century. His house was a great dark mansion at the end of Park Lane. I'd never heard of Wellington and had no reason to think he wasn't still alive. I didn't know then that he was the hero of Waterloo!

But soon enough I discovered that I wasn't going to be working for either a dead or a living Wellington anyway.

I walked the mile and a half to the big house along the Edgware Road and down Park Lane with the carts and cars and lorries and all the other usual bustle of the West End.

I found the house – couldn't miss it, it was so big – and waited at the front of the gates feeling very silly and very conspicuous.

Eventually a middle-aged woman who looked like the witch from *Snow White* approached me and said: 'Are you Kathleen?'

I said I was and she turned on her heel and snapped, 'Come on, be quick.'

So off I trotted after her, back across Park Lane and then across Piccadilly into Green Park. Why on earth is she taking me into the park? I wondered.

I had no idea where I was going or what I was doing, but I had a shilling in my bag which gave me confidence despite the fold of newspaper in my shoe to block up a hole. The rest of my rig-out was the best the flea market could muster and not a patch in sight. As I walked along like a dog behind its master I was half terrified and half confident.

Chapter 14

I was being taken to Spencer House, which was actually a palace in all but name. It was in spitting distance of Buckingham Palace yet surprisingly easy to miss, hidden behind its shrub- and tree-filled garden. But as I trotted along behind Mrs Snappy I knew nothing of any of this.

I'd never even heard of Buckingham Palace and had probably only thought about the king and queen once or twice in my whole life. My mum and dad had no interest in any of that sort of thing. The royal family might just as well have been living on Mars for all we cared.

And the truth is that the London poor only really started to care about the royal family during the Second World War when Queen Elizabeth stayed in London during the Blitz. After the First World War the royals were still unpopular because everyone knew they had changed their name from Battenberg because they were ashamed of being German.

All my parents cared about was football (my dad), the price of things and what the neighbours got up to. I reckon my mum and dad knew more about Queen

Victoria than about George V, who was in charge in 1926 when I started work.

So we crossed the park. It was summer I'm certain: I can still smell the lime trees. It wasn't till we were almost on top of it that I saw the house with its big pediment overlooking the park. We slipped down a narrow alleyway at the side of the house and came out in what I later discovered was St James's Street, the road that runs from Piccadilly down to St James's Palace.

The Spencers were related to the Churchills, the Grosvenors and just about every other grand family in the country. They had a vast estate in the country at Althorp in Northamptonshire but I was to work in their London house.

They had an enormous army of staff: maids, gardeners, a housekeeper, butler, half a dozen footmen, a dozen maids and hall boys galore, and on occasion the whole team, or major parts of it, would go up to the country or come down from the country to London.

I felt tiny as I walked through the vast kitchen and storerooms in the basement, still with that unfriendly head bobbing up and down mercilessly in front of me.

Actually Spencer House was very strangely situated really because we reached it from that narrow lane off St James's and there seemed no way in from the park front. Of course the park front was really all about showing off – it was a way for the family to say, 'Look at our house that almost faces the king's house! Look how important we are!' I don't think anyone used the front of the house as a way to go in and out, but it looked (from a distance) over a lane called Queen's Walk where the public were allowed to stroll.

Much later on my day off I walked out to see the house from the park and it was very grand indeed – pale grey stone, a huge pediment with statues along the top and long rows of symmetrical windows. The house survived both wars and is still there – I went to see it long after I retired.

As we marched through the corridors of that subterranean world I noticed everything: there were maids and skivvies bustling about everywhere, but with hardly any noise. I was astonished that the maids all seemed to have on different caps and the caps were all elaborate in different ways. That was my first and most lasting impression, though why I should have remembered such a trivial detail I don't know. Maids were given more lace on their caps as they went up the ranks. I also noticed that the maids and kitchen staff, the footmen and others as they bustled about still found time to nod and even bow to each other. It was to me despite my nerves and keeping my head down a most comical sight, like a black-and-white film badly lit and artificially speeded up.

This was my first taste of the rigid hierarchy below stairs. If a footman was rushing along with a big dish of beef it would still be necessary for him to nod a little bow to any senior footman he saw as he went along. Likewise junior maids nodded continually to senior maids. It actually looked like a madhouse of nodding and curtseying.

Chapter 15

I was such a lowly member of staff that the woman I was following didn't speak a word after that first exchange out in the street until she took me to a small room and snapped, 'Sit there.' She pointed to a wooden chair and then she left me.

Nowadays this sort of cold, horrible behaviour would be unimaginable. Even then it seemed a bit callous to me who was used to people being hard on each other. To walk all that way without even passing the time of day, without even looking at the person you were with – it seems unbelievable, but back then a young girl with no connections was not seen as deserving of any consideration at all. Good manners and kindness were reserved by many people for the better-off classes. Not everyone carried on like this and of course poor working-class people were sometimes treated with respect by the better-off but it was rare. There was also a deeply held view that the lower orders should always be grateful for what they had or what they'd been offered.

I didn't want to be a kitchen maid but the woman who bustled into the room a few minutes after I'd been left by the old scowler didn't give me the chance to say pretty much anything about what I wanted.

She said, 'It's three pounds a month. You'll be paid by the housekeeper. Start next week whichever day you can. Strictly – and I mean strictly – no followers.'

She paused then, unsure whether I knew what a follower was. She guessed I hadn't a clue what she was talking about and she was right.

'A follower is a boyfriend, a young man. Put all that out of your head and keep your eyes on your work or you'll be out. Mark my words.'

Here's another kindly one, I thought to myself.

'You haven't worked in a kitchen before, have you?' She didn't wait for an answer.

'Well, Cook will show you what to do. At the end of your first day one of the maids will show you where you'll sleep.'

And that was it. No mention of what I might want or not want, but that was the way then. The view of the world – but especially the staff in a big house like this – was that I was incredibly lucky that they had agreed to let me work in the house at all. It was a privilege.

My main memory of that first introduction to a great house was a scene I witnessed as I retraced my steps to the staff door, staring ahead all the time at the slightly hunched back of the woman who had brought me to the house.

47

We went along and I could hear only distant busy noises. Then without warning there was a terrific noise of shouting. It was a very violent kind of shouting and in the stone hall and the confined space it echoed about and was curiously frightening. We reached the big open doors that led into the kitchen. I was able to glance in and I saw the cook – I assumed it was the cook – holding a girl by the hair and shouting, 'I'll teach you a lesson you won't forget.' And with that she swung a big wooden spoon and repeatedly hit the girl across the back. Meanwhile the girl was trying to run away but with her hair grasped in the cook's hand she couldn't escape and instead half ran and half jumped in a circle trying to twist out of the way while continually being walloped with the spoon. I saw her hat crumpled and trodden on the ground.

My guide and I had both stopped in frozen amazement. The cook saw us and immediately let go. She looked about her in a slightly embarrassed way and brushed her apron down. All the other staff across the big room stood absolutely still.

A man in a dark, old-fashioned suit then appeared through a door on the other side of the kitchen. He gently pushed the girl who'd been beaten out of another door and led the cook quietly back to the centre of the room and bent to speak to her.

I saw no more because the woman I had been following, whose name I never discovered, glanced back at me at that instant and said, 'Come along you,' and moved off. I was almost shoved out a small door into the narrow road from which I'd arrived. The woman said, 'Go to the end of the lane and then left to the top.' She went back into the house and shut the door. She didn't even say goodbye. I walked up St James's to Piccadilly and then Park Lane in a daze.

Though wages had been mentioned there was nothing of holidays or hours of work. But what would have been the point of saying to a young girl entering service, 'Is that enough money?' or, 'Are you happy with the hours of work?'

There would have been no point because the system was absolutely rigid and no one had any choice – no one at the bottom anyway. It was slightly different for a good cook or butler and it later became a little better for maids and kitchen staff because by the 1930s they could leave and do something else if you made them work too hard. Just after the First World War and with the poverty of the 1920s domestic servants were still ten-a-penny so employers didn't have to be nice to them.

Once I started work I often heard employers and even senior staff saying that most junior servants didn't even deserve board and lodging, let alone wages on top of somewhere to sleep and something to eat.

'In my day it was much tougher, but it stood you in good stead' was just the sort of phrase you heard from older servants. And many employers thought that wages were a bad thing because servants were so ill-bred and ill-educated that giving them money was likely to lead to drinking since that was all they could be expected to think of doing with their money.

They would have laughed at the idea that we might have conversations with our friends or gone to a play or to the opera. If we weren't working we would get into trouble – that was the feeling – so even when we were middle-aged or elderly there was an idea that somehow we were like children, irresponsible and in need of firm control. Amazing isn't it?

On my first day at Spencer House I was told that on my afternoon off each Tuesday I was to go home to my family and not talk to any other servant who was having a half day on the same day, neither a servant from Spencer House nor from any other house round about. I was also told that meeting friends on my day off was not allowed. I didn't quite understand but since I had no friends outside a tiny area of Paddington I thought I could probably ignore it!

One of the servants explained to me that all this nonsense about not talking to anyone arose because the family hated the idea that the servants might go out with servants from other houses and gossip about their families. But what on earth a kitchen maid would ever know about the family that might lead to scandal I can't imagine. I suppose I did occasionally get to see Earl Spencer's underwear as it went in the wash and I might make comments about the quality of his linen or the size of his bottom. But other than that it was baffling.

So we were squeezed really and if you squeeze people down hard enough they will break out. Even in the most tightly controlled houses there was always an element of mischievousness.

Chapter 16

I discovered that work could be fun in my first week at Spencer House. I was allowed to talk to the hall boy who did all the most menial tasks for the upper servants – emptying their chamber pots, lighting and cleaning their fires and fetching and carrying all sorts of odds and ends. William, as he was called, clearly loved the fact that at last there was someone in the house he could impress.

'Bet you don't know anything about the family, do yer?'

I admitted I didn't.

'Richest in the country they are. Very big in the countryside, too, and the town. Bloomin' loaded. That's why they've got this house so close to the king's house over the way.'

He meant that we were a few hundred yards from Buckingham Palace.

William was an odd little chap. He had dark hair that lay flat on one side of his head and stuck up on the other, but even odder was that some days his hair stuck up on one side and some days on the other. It never stuck up all over his head and it was never all-over flat.

He had terribly thin arms I remember and looked about twelve. I remember the shock when I discovered he was nearly twenty. He always wore a waistcoat that buttoned up to his neck and even on his thin body it was terribly tight. He had very old -fashioned trousers too – they were what were called fall fronts with a flat piece of material across where you would expect the flies to be. They looked a bit like riding trousers, like jodhpurs. Those trousers were among a few oddities that Spencer House still had that had disappeared from most houses by the 1920s. They were handed down out of the old cupboards to new servants. The boys who'd originally worn those trousers were almost certainly long dead. The basement was full of things from the past: bits of carriages, coachmen's capes, and rows of leather fire buckets. The house even had its own fire engine, a handcart with a hose wound round a wheel and festooned with buckets and ladders.

I felt terribly sorry for William. He tried to be tough and chirpy and he copied some of the mannerisms of the older male servants but he wasn't very good at it and his swaggering and cheekiness somehow seemed a bit put on; but he was a terrific gossip who passed on all sorts of titbits from the junior footmen who'd got them from the maids or somewhere further up the ladder.

He'd often tell you something completely ordinary as if it was the most extraordinary thing.

'Do you know,' he would start every sentence, leaning towards you as if about to impart the juiciest bit of scandal in the whole history of gossip. 'Do you know. They've had extra milk every day for two weeks.'

He'd then stand back to gauge the effect of this remarkable piece of information.

Occasionally William had something that was genuinely worth listening to, but whatever it was if you didn't appear astonished he'd look really crestfallen. So whatever he said I would always reply, 'Good heavens!' or 'Well I never!' or 'Blimey, would you credit it?' He loved that.

And if you questioned him about the details of the story or asked, 'How do you know, how did you find out?' he was in ecstasies. He would tap the side of his shrivelled little nose and walk away with an enigmatic smile.

The head of the Spencer family at that time was Albert Edward John who had become the 7th Earl when he inherited the title very young in 1922. He had his own menservants whom we lowly types never saw or heard about, but the regular footmen made up his fires and they saw him now and then. They certainly told outrageous stories about him.

One footman who was a great favourite with almost all the other servants was known as James upstairs and Jimmy downstairs. He used to make us screech with laughter when the cook and housekeeper and other senior servants were locked away in the still room – the room where the cordials and more expensive preserves and other exotic foodstuffs were kept – or the butler's room, and we could get away with it.

He'd say, 'I don't mind His Lordship. Nice young man if only he wouldn't break wind at dinner.' Jimmy would keep a terrible straight face while saying this sort of thing and then look bewildered when we started to laugh. He'd say, 'What are you girls' – he pronounced it 'gewls' – 'laughing at? It's the truth. No word of a lie. Turn it up, ladies. Don't be the sceptical sort.'

Other stories that circulated about the earl were that he liked boys, but I think they only said that because he had a certain sort of look that seemed effeminate to men who had grown up in tougher circumstances. Upper-class men were always seen as milksops and weedy types. I saw a picture of the earl long after I'd left his employment and he did have a very girlish look when young but I put it down more to the fact that he was waited on hand and foot like a princess and, even in the army, he would have had a batman to carry him to the dining table and on and off the battlefield. It made him soft you see. My favourite story about the earl was that he was a bit absent-minded and footmen at dinner sometimes had to rush to the table to put out his napkin, which he often set on fire with a candle or a match. 'Where on earth would they be without us?' asked Jimmy with mock exasperation. Jimmy also told a story about the earl when he happened to see some ordinary soldiers swimming in a lake during the First World War. Apparently Spencer was astonished at how white and smooth the men's skin was. He just could not believe that the ordinary soldiers had skin as white as the aristocrats with whom he had only ever mixed. He had thought that the lower orders would be swarthy and hairy like apes!

Jimmy also told me that the Spencers, despite their wealth and position, were all bastards! He wasn't being rude – he meant they were literally bastards in the legal sense because they descended from some old king's backstairs work. I thought this was very unlikely but I found out he was right – the Spencers were descended from an illegitimate son of Charles II so they were no better than the rest of us after all.

Jimmy used to say, 'It's a right fiddle, innit? If I was a bastard I wouldn't get a job in the coal yard, but Bertie boy gets all the effing plums despite his ancestors. Funny old world! As long as yer a king's bastard it's all right.'

Jimmy had such a funny way with words. He had a few stock phrases he used again and again until you almost wanted to throw a bucket of water at him.

'Terrible weather today, Jimmy,' I'd say.

'Turn it up, Kat,' he'd reply.

'My dad just died, Jimmy.'

'Turn it up, Kat.'

'Half London has been bombed to bits.'

'Turn it up, Kat.'

You could never get anything else out of him at first, but bloody hell we used to try.

He was also one of those men who always tried it on with any and every girl he had anything to do with. He was always pinching my bottom and when I looked shocked or told him off he'd say, 'What? What did I do?' But it was very difficult to get cross with him and truth to tell I quite liked the attention. Most girls in service – well, the good-looking ones anyway – had a permanently flirty relationship with the male staff, or at least some of them, and they teased each other every chance they got. They only stopped when the old butler or the housekeeper was around. I was really angry with Jimmy very rarely, but I almost killed him when he shouted, 'Kat, come and feel this!' and dragged my hand down to the front of his trousers.

I shouted back at him, 'Now it's my turn – how does this feel?' And with that I stamped on his foot as hard as I could.

It was one of the great moments of my youth immediately after that to see a fully dressed footman hopping along the corridor yelping and holding his leg up in the air.

Chapter 17

In those early carefree days – and despite everything they were carefree – I found it hard to imagine being anything other than a lowly maid because the house-keeper job I really wanted seemed such a far-off possibility; but I saw the power the upper servants had and could easily imagine the money they earned. And because they were waited on by the youngest servants, their lives, in a bizarre way, seemed a bit like the lives of the people upstairs. It was impossible not to envy the upper servants because of the respect they received from all the other staff.

If we heard them coming along the corridor we'd all smooth down our uniforms and put on very serious faces – we'd start bustling around and adjusting our hair as if our lives depended on it. I eventually became a housekeeper but I hope I never became a stuffy old one because I enjoyed life. I was a terrible flirt as a girl so I could hardly have a go at the young ones when I grew old. When you are young and in service you have to find your fun where you can because most of the time life below stairs – or at least the work below stairs – is really boring! It was the gossip and the flirting that kept you sane.

On the other hand work, even in a kitchen, was a big improvement on home life. I felt I'd grown up enormously and I knew that work had to be taken seriously and that in an odd sort of way it was important. I don't mean looking after a load of layabout aristocrats was important, I mean getting on with your colleagues and getting things done on time and done properly. I got a lot of satisfaction from that because, as I've said, from my earliest days I liked to be organised.

So it was fun a lot of the time despite the ban on friends and boyfriends.

My favourite gossips were William and Jimmy. I only got the chance to talk to them now and then as I spent most of my time hurtling round the kitchen trying not to upset the cook who was my immediate and terrifying boss. I lost a lot of weight in my time in Spencer House because I was so determined never to get told off or get things wrong – and that meant you had to concentrate all the time.

Cook was in charge and despite what I'd seen of her on my interview day she wasn't really such a bad old thing. She quickly realised I wanted to get things right and we got on very well as a result. I think she came to rely on me. She was very disappointed when, after a few months, I told her that I didn't really want to stay in the kitchen. She thought I'd be a good cook – and as it turned out I was a good cook for a short while – but it was organising the spoons and saucepans and making sure everything was ready when needed that interested me, not really the cooking itself.

Much as I think Cook liked me she had a temper, so I decided I would make myself indispensable to her. When she realised what I was doing she softened a bit and I came to know some of her difficulties.

She had a strong, broad face, with a sort of soft pudgy nose and sharp thin lips and no hair at all – or at least that's how she seemed to me – and she wore an unusual cap that covered her head and she never seemed to take it off. She had such a weight of responsibility because huge sides of beef and lamb, tons of game and vegetables, went through her hands and all had to reach the dining table in the best possible condition, especially when they were entertaining, which was a lot of the time. She was also constantly afraid that she would be replaced by a French chef because French chefs were all the rage then if you could afford them.

She used to say under her breath, 'I've half a mind to leave them to Monsieur Frog's Leg and let them eat pigs' balls in a bloody ragout.'

I'm sure the earl had no idea that we were all downstairs giving up the best part of our lives for the comfort of him and his family. They had been brought up not to consider us.

I found most of the work except the washing-up hard but not too hard. I got round the problem of sore hands by pinching a bit of lard from the pantry every other day or so and then rubbing it on my skin. Worked a treat, and you needed something like that because kitchen work was so hard on the skin and I didn't want to look like an old granny before my time.

I was very vain. In fact I was frequently told off for looking at myself all the time in the window glass and the door glass. When I thought my face was looking a bit dry I even dabbed a bit of lard on my cheeks – I couldn't afford face cream and lard was just as good, though I'm sure it made me smell like steak and kidney pudding.

Throughout my years in service I found that it was always a good idea to ask yourself: Is there a better way to do this? And in the kitchen at the Spencers' I worked out several ways to speed up the process of cleaning the pans and getting the knives sharpened more often. Kitchen work is so much easier with good equipment.

Within a few months of starting work I'd started to think about moving – I was so desperate to get on and, besides, all the other servants were constantly talking about looking for a new situation, as they used to put it. I was determined to do it because you never got anywhere staying in the same house. That much I had quickly learned. But then, without me doing much to make anything change, everything changed.

Chapter 18

In the summer of 1926 there was a huge change at Spencer House that put paid to Cook's plans for me and parted me forever from William and Jimmy and the maids I'd got to know. The Spencers decided to move permanently away from London and to let the old house.

So my first job lasted less than a year, although I did get something most servants were never offered. I got a chance to look at the amazing richness of the rooms upstairs.

I'd been dawdling in the servants' hall with one of the housemaids, a girl called Mamie, during my bit of free time in the afternoons when the senior footman appeared and said to both of us, 'Oi, don't suppose you two fancy a look-round upstairs? We're all out on our ears in a few weeks anyway so can't do any harm.'

I jumped at the chance without even thinking about what he'd said – I mean that bit about us all being out on our ears. I just didn't take in what he meant. Mamie, who was the shyest creature I ever met, immediately disappeared without a word. But I followed the senior footman. I suspect Mamie might have known a bit more about the footman than I did because as we set off he said, 'What do I get for showing you round?'

'What do you want?' I replied, thinking in my innocence that he might ask me to pinch something for him from the kitchen.

'I'll have a kiss then,' he said and without a word he grabbed me, pulled me up to him and kissed me very hard. He also pushed his tongue into my mouth which I half enjoyed and half thought disgusting.

I was dazed while this went on as no one had ever done anything like this to me before. I could feel the breath being squeezed out of me and then he let go. I should have slapped him I suppose but I was too amazed and there and then I think I realised how much power a girl can have over men if she chooses to use it. It was a feeling I enjoyed.

'Come on then, you've had your kiss,' I said. 'Off we go.'

But he said he wanted another kiss. I said yes and we got down to it again but then he did something I really thought was a bit too much. He got his hand between us and gave one of my breasts a really hard and very mechanical sort of squeeze and it bloody hurt. That seemed to galvanise me and I gave him an almighty shove that nearly knocked him over. But I wasn't afraid at all. I just laughed and said, 'Try that again and I'll have my dad up here after you.'

I don't think he was the least bit concerned that I'd really do anything of the sort because that's what every girl said when she was pestered. Either that or it was the brother who would come and sort things out. Anyway we both laughed and he took me upstairs into a world of such ridiculous luxury that I couldn't take it all in. The ceilings in one room were enormously high with decorative plaster and gilt everywhere and a vast painted scene in a centre panel. There were highly decorated tables, ornate chairs and tables, inlaid cupboards, sofas and yards of thick curtains held up by massive poles. Everything seemed to me to be on an almost superhuman scale – the fireplace would have taken two or three hundredweight of coal and every surface was covered with expensive silver and glass. A gigantic window looked over towards Buckingham Palace. If this was what a king's bastard could expect I was all for it! But it also looked a bit like showing off to me because the rooms were so uncomfortable, like a museum.

The senior footman used to grab me pretty much every time he saw me after that first occasion and at first I liked the attention but I worried the others would start talking about me so I decided to put a stop to it. He grabbed me one day and I grabbed him as hard as I could where it hurt and squeezed much harder than he'd ever squeezed me! He left me alone after that, although I used to tease him and say, 'Don't you fancy a squeeze then?' He would give me a sickly smile. I think he was a little afraid of me. I certainly wasn't afraid of him and in fact I hardly remember ever being afraid of anyone.

I think I was unusual in other ways too. For a start I wasn't in the least prudish, which a lot of girls were at that time. After my first kiss I quickly got the hang of it and I liked it – I didn't think there was anything dirty about it. It was exciting and boys were exciting because they wanted us girls so badly. We were like drink to them and they couldn't get enough of us. I thought, I can make something of this. But I knew from the start that the one thing you could never do was get pregnant. Getting pregnant was a disaster from which there was almost no chance of recovery because you'd lose your job and you'd need money to get through the weeks, maybe months, during which you couldn't work because of the baby. The well-off could always find a doctor prepared to give them an abortion in those days – it was called 'having a D and C', meaning dilatation and curettage – and we all knew about it and regretted that we didn't have the money for it if need be. You had to get rid of it if you did get pregnant because if you were having someone's baby and they'd run off and left you no one else would have you – why would they? Why choose a pregnant girl who was just going to cost you money when you'd be looking after someone else's kid as well? So I knew I had to be careful and not get carried away.

But sex definitely reared its ugly head in my next job and in a very odd way!

Chapter 19

A few days after that incident with the senior footman we discovered that the rumours were right after all. We were formally told by the housekeeper that the Spencers were giving up their London home for good and going back to Althorp. Only some of the servants would go with them and the London house was to be let as offices. In the end I don't think the family even bothered to keep a flat in the huge house, but, either way, a few weeks later I found myself out of work.

Chapter 20

As I've said, sex was to be the cause of ructions in my next job. I was a very good-looking girl and until I was thirty – we aged quickly in those days! – I was pestered a lot and gawked at by boys and men of all ages, but I always seemed well able to deal with it. I had naturally blonde hair and lots of it, a small straight nose and blue eyes and you'd be amazed at how men react to that combination. I was also of very slim build in those days – we all were, what with walking everywhere and working twelve-hour days!

But it used to amaze me how much more attention you got as a blonde compared to a brunette – which is why so many women have always dyed their hair. I didn't have to so I was lucky and the girls I worked with often said to me, 'Get a rich husband. That's the way to get on. You've got the looks so don't let yourself go at any old price.'

All girls thought in terms of marriage back then, but most wanted to marry for love. We were probably more romantic than any generation before or since because the cinema – especially the cinema when the talkies came in – gave us romantic notions. We all dreamed of a dashing young man with a car and a huge fortune whisking us off to the south of France and a big house in the country, but it was all nonsense and I knew it. No one really rich was ever going to marry a common girl however good-looking she was. But this didn't bother me because I thought the so-called rich young men I occasionally came across were all putting it on anyway. If you met someone in a bar or even a tea shop the first thing they would do if they wanted to chat you up was boast about their background, their connections, their important job and the fact that their father was hugely rich or had been to Eton.

It was almost always a load of old balls.

They played a game too and hoped a few girls would fall for it and be so dazzled that they'd sleep with them on the promise of future marriage – a promise that disappeared after they got what they wanted. So it was around this time that I thought I would play them at their own game. I'd keep stringing them along and get what I could out of them and just occasionally sleep with one I really fancied and only then if he agreed to be careful.

Boots the Chemists sold condoms openly until the early 1920s and then pressure from the stupid Church stopped them and they became much harder to get. You had to go up to Soho to get them, and Christ you got some dirty looks in the sleazy little shops that sold them, still illegally I think. But I made sure I had them just in case I felt like throwing caution to the wind! And you could never rely on a bloke having one. You had to keep a cool head to make the silly buggers use them because they never wanted to.

But sex was the last thing on my mind – well, almost the last thing – in 1926 because I had to get a job after being left high and dry by the Spencers. The country was in a right state what with the General Strike and low wages and high unemployment, and the truth was I liked getting paid even though it wasn't much – like my dad I wanted to have a jingle in my pocket. And I loved the fact that I was independent now. I would have died rather than slink off home to Paddington. Luckily, although factory jobs had declined in the 1920s there was a shortage of servants so despite the general gloom it was a bit easier for domestics than for other people.

I hated the idea of going back to an agency because I didn't want to be treated like a sack of wool or a bit of livestock so I asked around and bought a copy of the local newspaper. This was during my last week at Spencer house so I was cutting it fine – but then I was only sixteen!

I was astonished at how many jobs were on offer. I thought, You are in clover, my girl. There were pages and pages of small cramped-looking ads and for all sorts of jobs from lowly kitchen maids to highfalutin cooks, housekeepers and butlers. But I noticed all the ads were written in the same way. They asked for experienced, sober staff who were hard-working and, above all, respectable, because the advertisements always emphasised that the employers themselves were extremely respectable. It's impossible now to imagine the weight of that word 'respectable'. To be thought respectable by your friends and neighbours was the greatest thing imaginable if you were middle class even though upper-class people would have laughed at the idea that respectability was important. In fact the desire to be seen as respectable was a sure sign that you were horribly middle class – although of course I only found that out after years of working for the upper classes.

But one word was even more important than respectable. This was the word 'gentleman'. Like 'respectable' it was hugely important when I was young, yet fifty years later both words had lost all their power to hurt. Advertisements for staff would always say: 'Required for gentleman's household, a respectable housemaid'. Or 'A Lady of the utmost respectability requires a sober maid of all work'. And so on.

Even at age sixteen, I knew that 'respectable' and 'gentlemen' were words used by any – and everyone who wanted to seem better than they were. Throughout my career I saw the truth of this again and again. People always exaggerated their status and the gold standard for a man was to be able to put on a form the word 'gentleman', which back then meant a funny mixture of being well educated and, above all, of independent means. Even doctors were looked down on as little more than tradesmen because they worked for money. Gentlemen typically owned land or were lawyers or MPs because being an MP was more of a hobby back then when it was unpaid. This is why the Earl Spencer for whom I had worked eventually entered Parliament. It was like an extension of their London clubs; a place where they met all the other people with whom they'd been at school.

Similarly a lady was someone with an independent income who could play the piano and best of all had 'come out'. That was the funny ceremony when upper-class girls were introduced to the Queen at Court and then married off to equally upper-class boys at a series of balls that only the upper classes were ever invited to.

So I ignored the advertisements that had nothing of interest in them beyond these words and decided that moving out of London might be fun for a while. I didn't want to go too far but all the talk in Spencer House among the staff who were moving to Althorp made me think I might like to try a change of scene. After a bit of dithering I answered an advertisement for a kitchen maid's job in a big house in Leicestershire. I hadn't a clue where or what Leicestershire was but the appeal of the unknown was strong. And though I didn't really want to go back in the kitchen I needed a job and I had no experience at anything else.

My letter of application brought a quick response. I wasn't asked for an interview, but instead received a letter saying that, as I had good references, they would take me on trial for a month and if all went well I could stay on permanently.

And so I left London and went to a strange little feudal village where I was to work until I was in my mid-twenties. It was one of the oddest places I have ever been and there is nowhere like it today but I was to learn everything I needed to know to rise from maid to housekeeper.

I remember my first journey to Leicestershire as if it were yesterday. If you travelled by train then, as I did, you would have enjoyed an experience far different from rail travel in more recent times.

You could travel first, second or third class and of course there was a huge difference in price and comfort between the three. Oddly, too, even if you had the money for first class you wouldn't dare go in it if you weren't the right sort of person dressed in the right sort of clothes. Your whole bearing and attitude would give you away and other passengers would give you the cold shoulder and make you feel horribly uncomfortable. So I went third class. I knew my place!

Chapter 21

The train arrived at what looked like the station at the end of the world. Along the platform was a tiny one-roomed station office, red-tiled and with a trickle of smoke coming from its tiny chimney. Round about, as far as I could see, were fields and hedges and a distant church spire. I was relieved to be off the train as the third-class seats were hard and a boy in the same compartment had been sick just twenty minutes into the journey. His mother had hardly reacted, with no apology to the other passengers or any attempt to clear it up, so the rest of us had suffered the terrible smell in silence.

I waited a few moments and watched the train disappear up the line. I'd received a letter from the housekeeper. She told me that I should wait on the station platform and someone would come to pick me up. Well, I waited and waited and no one came. I was a city girl and standing on that platform was the loneliest moment of my life. Some people would have loved the quiet and emptiness, the green fields stretching away broken only by hedges and small woods; but to me this was an empty, slightly frightening landscape.

Eventually I knocked timidly on the door of the station house. A short man in dark blue serge and a peaked cap opened the door. He can't have been more than five feet tall. He squinted up at me.

'You'll be expecting Mrs Jennings,' he said. He took a large, very dirty-looking gunmetal watch out of his pocket – it was almost the size of a small clock – and said, 'She'll be ten more minutes, more or less, I'd say.'

I said nothing in reply and he must have thought I was an idiot because I just stared at him. He smiled and said in a cheery voice, 'You can wait in here.'

I noticed that his watch, which I couldn't take my eyes off, only had a minute hand, so how he knew the time I hadn't a clue. But I smiled back at him and said 'Thank you' in what I hoped was an equally cheery voice.

The little station hut was very curious. It looked like a labourer's cottage rather than a place where someone worked. There was a small fire in the tiny grate with a black kettle on a hob at the side and a half-broken-down armchair into which the little stationmaster gingerly lowered himself as if he had terrible backache. Why a stationmaster would be needed for a station as small as this I have no idea but all stations had staff in those days except what were called 'halts', which were almost unofficial stops in that you had to request the guard to ask the driver to stop if you wanted to get off or on.

Having beckoned me into the one-room cottage the stationmaster pointed to a battered, upholstered chair on the opposite side of the fireplace. I sat there and no doubt confirmed his view that I was an imbecile by continuing to smile but saying nothing.

We stared in uncomfortable silence at each other. I looked around and saw there was a picture of Queen Victoria on the wall above the fireplace and an old poster from the First World War which had never been taken down.

After a while he said, 'All the servants from the house come through here. I see them all one time or another. Either going down or coming up.'

'Are there many servants at the house?' I asked.

'Many. Too many,' he said, and he gave me a piercing look, 'and they're always coming and going. When I first came here servants was born and bred here but not any more. Lots of incomers now. Lots of them.'

And with that he looked directly at me in a way that made me feel as if I'd committed a terrible sin in coming to Leicestershire. I wasn't offended a bit because like a lot of London people I slightly looked down on country people and I thought, Well how much do you know about anything, mister? But I was surprised that he clearly knew where I was going and why I was there. It was the first thing I learned about my new life – you couldn't move in this part of Leicestershire without almost everyone round about knowing.

I'd just finished nodding and smiling at his last remark when the door opened – there was no knock – and a young man in a heavy corduroy suit entered the room and took his hat off.

'You're for the house?' he said.

'I am, yes. Yes, I am,' I gibbered.

The young man nodded, turned and walked out of the little house without a word to anyone. I nodded to the stationmaster, thinking that this nodding business was clearly the main way they communicated round there, and followed the new arrival out and back on to the platform.

I got to know many of the local villages during my time in Leicestershire and what would amaze anyone going back to that time was how quiet they were. With few cars and the only jobs those on the land there was none of the noise and bustle of later times. To me every day in the countryside seemed like a Sunday, since back in London that was the only quiet day we had each week.

The young man threw my bag into the back of what looked to me like a farm cart.

This is a nice beginning! I thought.

Having been almost completely dumb in front of the stationmaster the young man suddenly started to talk once we were in the gig.

'You're from London?' he said. 'What's it like then? I hear it would take a week to walk across it and the smoke and noise is terrible, motor cars everywhere. Why you up here then? We got any number of

Londoners up here so it must be bad down there. I feel bad for them having to come all this way. They're a funny lot too, Londoners. Always going the wrong way up the lanes and getting theirselves lost, but they're drawn to us they are. And they speak with forrin accents. I suppose there are a lot of forriners in London?'

And on he continued for the two or three miles to the house. From what he said I imagined the house would be thick with servants from Paddington and everywhere else in London, but within a few days I found I was the only Londoner there, in the village and anywhere else within five miles! Like a lot of country people he just said the first thing that came into his head and deliberately exaggerated to liven things up a bit.

A lot of the family are still in the area so I'd better be careful what I say, but the old house was demolished in the mid-1930s. It was a huge place and the family who owned it also owned the whole village and all the outlying farms and all the cottages. They had owned everything for more than four hundred years.

It was also unusual in that the family had never had to sell any land or other possessions to pay the new taxes that were coming in for the very rich. The family still had enough cash to carry on as they'd done in the 1800s and earlier. You could see how slow they were to change from the number and type of servants they employed.

The footmen all wore black-and-yellow livery, the butler was still in a frock coat, and there were still maids – I mean maids who worked in the still room. There were also laundry maids because none of the washing was sent out, housemaids, kitchen maids, two ladies' maids, scullery maids and several maids who seemed to do a bit of everything. There was also a team of gardeners and odd-job men and even an estate carpenter.

'We have a prodigious staff,' said the cook when I was taken down to the huge kitchen and introduced to her. Everything in fact was prodigious. The kitchen was like a great hall; it would even have dwarfed the kitchen in the Spencers' London house.

The kitchen might have been big, but heavens above, it was also very inefficient and its size seemed to have more to do not with the number of people for whom it catered but with the number of staff needed to fit in it! And it was full of old-fashioned equipment dating back forty years or more.

There were wires and pulleys hanging down and nailed and screwed up everywhere on the walls and ceiling. The gleaming black range – a sort of old-fashioned cooker – must have been fifteen feet long and there were batteries of huge ovens opposite, all with heavy black cast-iron doors shining in the fire-light like polished coal.

Nothing had changed in that kitchen since the 1880s if not earlier. I knew this because as the days in my new job turned into weeks I noticed many of the cast-iron doors had dates on them. One said 1842, which shows you just what we were dealing with!

They had no labour-saving devices at all in that kitchen and there was no gaslight, only oil lamps and logs and coal for the house fires and the range and ovens.

All the servants' rooms and even the small rooms and pantries, the cupboards and closets, had been built on what seemed to me a vast scale and though there were the usual rules about bowing to senior servants and not daring to look at any member of the family, it was a tolerant house; partly, I think, because many if not most of the staff had known each other at the local school, which meant their families also knew each other. There were exceptions – some of the maids had come from further afield in Rutland and Lincolnshire and one of the lady's maids was Scottish, but that was it really. The rest were locals which is why I stood out like a sore thumb. But it was my London background and the idea that Londoners were some-how sharper than other people that helped eventually to give me my chance.

Chapter 22

My first few weeks were lonely and I missed the streets of London and especially Paddington which was a dump when you were there but somehow seemed much nicer when you were one hundred and fifty miles away.

I had a room with the other kitchen maid and two junior housemaids in the attic, and if you went up to the attic on your own there was a better than even chance you would get lost. The joke in the house was that one maid had tried to find her room without help when she first arrived and she had never been seen again! I think that might have been a bit of an exaggeration but it was certainly true that the attic rooms seemed to branch off in every direction and many of the corridors were in permanent darkness for they were unlit by lamp or window.

Though I worked in that house for six years and more I never really fathomed my way round the attic. There were two sets of servants' stairs and each brought you to a part of the attic that seemed big enough on its own to fill the whole top of the house; yet you knew that the other staircase took you to another part of the house where the attic was just as big and just as meandering.

All the servants' rooms were sparsely furnished, but on all except the coldest days they were reasonably warm because the heat rose to the attics from all the blazing fires down below. So although they did not have their own fires they were not as bad as they might have seemed. The senior servants had bigger rooms in the basement for sure but they always seemed rather damp and miserable to me. Up top we had small windows and as one of my fellow maids said, 'At least we know we're much closer to the sun and to heaven up here,' which was true. Something I didn't like was that all the maids in a room had to share a wardrobe and the furniture was hideous – all the beds were made of what resembled iron piping, like something you'd expect mad people in an asylum to sleep in.

Netta, who was one of the housemaids I shared with, became my great friend in Leicestershire. She was an innocent thing I thought but everyone liked her because she never had a bad word to say about anyone. Nessa, the other housemaid who shared our room, was much sharper-tongued with everyone except Netta.

I was astonished from the outset that the two of them found it a constant source of amusement that they had similar names. Almost every day they would go through a little routine in which they pretended they couldn't remember who was who. It must be a country thing, I thought. In other respects Nessa was genuinely very funny. She would make great jokes about the village girls.

'My fanny's in a right old state today,' she would say. 'It's the butler's blue eyes that done it. It's been so long I think I've healed over!' I wish I could remember her other phrases – they were always very rude and very funny.

One freezing night after we had all gone to bed exhausted – it was during my first winter at the house – I was about to drop off to sleep when I heard a voice.

'My tits are bloody freezing!' It was sharp-tongued Nessa. There was a pause and then Netta and I began screeching with laughter that lasted a good ten minutes.

'What are you two laughing about?' said Nessa, who pretended to be offended. 'I'm sure you've heard the word "tits" before. And they are bloody freezing. If you don't stop laughing I'll come up your end and give you a good warming!'

As my first winter came and weeks of hard frost and ice set in I began to think that Leicestershire was the most godforsaken place on earth. I regularly saw birds lying dead on the drive up to the road – they'd frozen while roosting and just dropped to earth. Even the huge fires in the family rooms below the servants' rooms failed to take the edge off the cold although they were kept going almost continually.

One night towards the Christmas of my first year I was shivering beneath the blankets when Netta shook me gently and asked if she could get into bed with me as she was freezing. In those innocent days I saw no reason to refuse so I said yes and ten minutes later we were fast asleep and probably warmer than anyone else in the house.

'Or in the country,' said Netta the next morning. After that she slept with me every night and I've never slept better before or since.

I say Nessa had a sharp tongue, which is true, but she was also very kind if a little blunt sometimes. When Netta used to climb into my bed Nessa would shout across, 'Are you two at it again? Why don't I ever get invited?' She herself hated to be touched or hugged or kissed because for several years during her childhood one of her many uncles had regularly come to the house and, whenever he got the chance, had jammed his hand in her knickers.

In the gossipy way country houses were run in those days rumour spread that Netta and I were up to no good and about a month later I was called in to see the housekeeper.

'I don't quite know how they do things in London but we are not the same here,' she said.

I looked blankly at her. Hadn't a clue what she was talking about.

'I think you know what I mean.'

'Is it something to do with my work?' I said.

'You are being deliberately silly,' she said.

I looked blank again.

She stood up and walked to the big window that looked down across the parkland.

'This is very difficult for me you know,' she said. 'But if it does not stop I will have to ensure you sleep in a room on your own.'

Suddenly I knew what she was talking about.

Before I could think, I said, 'But we only share my bed because it is so cold.'

'I don't want to hear. It is disgusting,' she said, still staring out through the window and carefully keeping her back to me. I just glimpsed the side of her face and she was absolutely beetroot red. I'd gone red too. I thought perhaps she meant sleeping with Netta was disgusting from a hygiene point of view, or maybe she was worried we were too heavy for the bed. I just couldn't think why sleeping together was such a problem.

I had no idea that she could be thinking anything else.

I said: 'Well, I won't sleep with Netta any more if it is against the rules.'

'We will say no more about it then. Thank you. You may go.'

She said all that without turning round so I stood up and quietly left the room.

When I told Netta she was really upset and despite her soft ways she said, 'She's horrible. We're not hurting anyone. I was always cold before.'

But that was the end of it. What could we do?

When I told Nessa, she said, 'Of course. She thinks you're having sex with each other, you dirty lesbeans.' That was how she pronounced it – 'lez beans'. I'd never heard the word before, and I had never heard of the idea of women having sex with each other.

Nessa said, 'Don't worry. Half the maids in the country are having sex with each other. Just be a bit more careful, can't you?'

'But we weren't having sex,' I said.

'Go on. Pull the other one,' she said.

And I never was able to convince her, but Netta and I slept in separate beds after that.

Chapter 23

Netta and Nessa were my friends and looking back I'm surprised how easy it was to make such friends and so quickly. I always felt that children make friends easily, and teenagers – and I was still a teenager at this time – but it's never again so easy as we grow older, perhaps because as we get older we only really live in the past. All my memories of Nessa and Netta are happy ones, but the same cannot be said of my memories of other people in the house.

The family were definitely very odd. In one way or another all my employers were to be either eccentric or mad or both, but it was particularly noticeable in that big old house in Leicestershire.

Several things struck me as very strange in my first few weeks. I was warned by Cook that I would find things very different from the London house where I had worked and how right she was.

My first Sunday came around – we were given every other Sunday as a holiday – and I got up as usual at six o'clock and dressed and got downstairs as quickly as I could ready to prepare the breakfast things.

At eight o'clock the cook told me to stop and come to the servants' hall. I was expecting to be told off for some terrible new thing I'd done without realising it, but no. When I got there all the other servants were already gathered together. The footmen were in their best coats, brass buttons shining like gold. The maids were all in freshly laundered white caps and aprons. The cook, butler and housekeeper were hovering nearby. This must be something very important, I thought. Moments later we trooped up the curving servants' stairs and walked in file, and strictly in order of importance, through the door that led to the great entrance hall of the house.

We lined up in three rows stretching from the bottom of the huge staircase to just inside the front door. I was so busy marvelling at the size of the staircase, the life-size marble heads and statues and the ancient flags hanging from the walls high up that it took a nudge in the ribs from Nessa to get my mind back on what was happening.

Slowly down the stairs came the family, all in their Sunday best. I had never seen any of them before because the kitchen maid was less than nothing in a house like this. They looked pretty undistinguished to me. The boss, who after all only had a knighthood, came first, followed by Her Ladyship, all nodding feathers and bosom and a dozen or so younger people I assumed were their children. Then came an extremely elderly couple and one or two middle-aged men and women.

What a bunch they were! All wearing clothes at least twenty years out of date, the women in long skirts almost to the ground, the men in waistcoats and Victorian trousers. The overwhelming impression they gave was that they were made of clothes – you could hardly see the humans for black silk, long coats, boots, gloves and sticks and all the other excess bits and pieces the rich in those days thought essential.

When they had assembled facing us servants across the hall the head of the house – who seemed eerily tall to me – lifted his hand like a preacher. There was silence. A footman immediately approached, did a little bow and handed over an ancient-looking Bible. This was placed on a wooden stand and then the baronet read for ten minutes. With that done the family traipsed back up their stairs and we traipsed down ours. During the reading I watched the family's faces. They looked very uncomfortable for those few minutes when we all had to stand together, and the huge gulf between servant and master seemed to narrow for an instant. It was clearly their idea that, before God at least, we should look as if we were all vaguely equal – although clearly the experience was painful for the family, whose faces remained rigid throughout.

This was to be a regular Sunday event from now on and what a farce it was. It certainly put me off religion for many years.

'Why we have to get up early on the Lord's day to listen to all this rubbish I just don't know,' said Nessa. 'It's supposed to be a day of rest so why can't we all just stay in bed?'

I barely understood any of the readings on that first or any other Sunday and neither did any of the other servants as far as I could tell. Their version of the Bible was two hundred years out of date at least and the language so old-fashioned we were mystified, but no doubt the family thought it was all very improving for us.

After the gathering in the hall, it was back to the kitchen as fast as your legs could carry you. Breakfast was now everyone's concern. I rustled up the numerous implements and pots and pans and put them in the right places.

Whether it was breakfast, dinner or tea I was always astonished at the amount of food we cooked and at the huge number of spoons and bowls and other dishes that were necessary to cook and serve the simplest thing. Before and after breakfast the deliveries for that day would arrive. Every few minutes it seemed there would come a knock at the door and a man or more often a boy in an apron would appear with a whole side of a pig, a basket of eggs or vegetables, sacks of potatoes, or birds hanging by their necks and still with their feathers on.

The gardener's boy would arrive with mushrooms and other garden stuff such as herbs or fruit.

Some of all this would be cut up and cooked as soon as it arrived, the rest would be kept on hand for lunch or dinner. Almost everything was fresh because there was no way to keep anything cold.

Sometime before or occasionally just after breakfast there would be a knock at the kitchen door. Immediately a hush would fall and all the maids would immediately stand still. The lady of the house would enter while we maids stood demurely against the giant range. Her Ladyship would explain to Cook that people were coming or the family wanted one dish or menu or another. Then she would leave and we would get back to work, rushing through steam, chopping endless vegetables, dashing to collect things that Cook needed in a split second.

Chapter 24

Weeks, months and then finally years passed in that kitchen and I settled into a pattern broken only by my afternoons off when I would get the bus into town, and my alternate Sundays. On these days I would lie on my bed and read or go for walks. There wasn't much point going to town because in those days everything was shut on a Sunday.

After the crowds of London and no space at all that was not filled with people I found the quiet lanes and fields enormously enjoyable once I'd got over my initial shock.

And as I walked along, sometimes mile after mile if the weather was fine, I enjoyed the way the local people would tip their hats to me or more often stop for a chat. They were remarkably open in a way that London people were not. Londoners loved to chat but they were more suspicious of strangers I think. Country people saw someone coming along the road as a chance to talk in a world where talk was often the only entertainment because it cost nothing. It was gentle and enjoyable to me, but it also could be a bloody nuisance because you could never get away from some people.

I remember particularly one walk when an old man I'd seen several times stopped me and said he would accompany me along the road. At first I was nervous as in London you'd have instantly thought this was a thief or lunatic but the old man had a gentle, lilting way of talking that was very reassuring and entertaining and he made my walk far more enjoyable in the end. It's hard to recall the wonderful rambling, twinkling tone of his conversation but it was something like this:

'Morning, missy.'

'Morning,' I replied.

'What's the news from the house? How's Cook?'

'She's well, thank you.'

'I remember her as a girl. Very cool. Very cool, she was but saucy too. Very saucy. Used to get herself in a terrible pickle over her brothers and sisters. She was a mother to them all. A mother. But they are a terrible family for the bottle. Terrible.'

By now we'd have covered maybe one hundred yards along the gravelled road.

He'd then ask me if I was enjoying myself or he'd ask about my family, but before I could reply he'd be off again about himself or some character in the village.

'I have a terrible ulcer on this leg. Now what's interesting about this ulcer is that till recently it was on the other leg. A mystery is what my health is. And the good Lord knows I've looked after myself. Very little in the way of drink and never talking about people behind their backs but I'm still afflicted. And I have these terrible sores on my hands. Now why would I get those, I ask you, when I've worked hard all my life and the hands are like iron or they should be.'

On and on he would go, but he was a sweet old thing and typical of the villagers, who would stick to you like glue if they got the chance. I thought then and I think it still that country people are lonely in a way that city people never are.

Then there was Willy. To get away from Willy you would have to dodge into a field or make an excuse and pretend you were late and then run off and of course he was too old to chase you! If he met you a week later he would show no sign at all that he was offended by your running off the last time he saw you.

Half a mile from the big house was the village shop which was run by Mrs Eades. Mrs Eades was a widow and her small shop was filled with the most extraordinary range of goods. She sold eggs, butter and pegs, nails and firewood, sacks, sweets, socks, smocks, newspapers, shoes, boots, tins of polish, potatoes, bolts of cloth and bags of coal. She was a one-woman department store – she even had a second-hand department and a bookshop!

Most of her produce seemed to be hanging from bits of string that criss-crossed the tiny room where she sat in a chair with her cat on her lap and smoking dark brown cigarettes.

I spent a lot of my wages in Mrs Eades' shop and usually on sweets or ribbons. Now Mrs Eades sold huge amounts of ribbon in those days for the simple reason that girls were always convinced that ribbon was a cheap and highly effective way to transform their looks. They couldn't afford new dresses or hats or shoes so they made do with brightly coloured ribbon. Tied into your hair it made you look brighter-eyed and lively somehow, and it made you forget the awful bloody uniforms we had to wear most of the time.

In an old-fashioned area like rural Leicestershire, ribbon was one of those things that were frowned on for servant girls – but we bought our ribbon anyway and hid it or wore it on Sundays when we were well out of sight of the house.

At various times in my first few months I was told off for wearing ribbon, for singing and for whistling, but the fact that they watched us this closely and took a day-to-day interest not just in our work but in every-thing we did and everywhere we went was all part of the old-style, feudal nature of the place.

Chapter 25

The family owned all the land round about the house, all the farms and all the tenanted cottages, and their relationship with their tenants was not just a question of collecting the rent. Tenants still had to do as the landowner wanted. He hunted across anyone's and everyone's land, invited his friends to shoot over fields and woods that were strictly speaking the property of his tenants because they paid rent for them, and he expected all his tenants to turn up at the midsummer fête. If pheasants and deer were eating the tenants' crops or their roses, the tenants had to put up with it.

Most feudal of all was the rent table. This was a huge, battered, circular table that seemed to have been designed to make the business of paying rent less obviously financial. I think the idea was to reduce the sense in which the landowner was actually a business-man. Landowners hated references to money because financial considerations were somehow beneath them, so twice a year – on Lady Day and Michaelmas, I think – the tenants would file into a special part of the

95

house where the 'factor', the estate manager, had his office and they would put their rent in cash in a series of special drawers around the edge of the rent table. Strictly speaking it was called a drum table, I think. The tenants having put their money in the numerous drawers would then file out, heads bowed and looking suitably humbled by the grand surroundings. It was all done very discreetly though of course the amount of cash they had put in the drawers was carefully checked by the factor once they'd left. The head of the family or his son was always there but watching from a distance rather than sitting at the table.

It was the factor's job to turn the table one drawer at a time and empty each drawer and count the money. One thing that made the tenants' visit a little less stressful was that each was offered a glass of port after the money had been deposited. That too was part of the tradition.

Because life on the estate was so unchanging there was a lot of petty interference which I resented. I went along with it all on the basis that as I really couldn't beat them I would have to join them. By that I mean I never had to be told something twice. If they said 'No singing!' I stopped singing. If they said 'No ribbon!' I stopped wearing it except when I was on my day off. Inwardly I felt this was all very unfair, but I also thought, If I get to the top I will then be able to at least bend the rules a bit.

I got my first chance to show them what I could do after I had been in Leicestershire for about eighteen months. I can remember the day as if it was yesterday.

I was busy in the kitchen when I noticed that Cook was not dodging about as she usually was. She was leaning on the kitchen block – a great slab of wood on legs that we used to cut the meat on – and staring at a long strip of paper. After a bit I said to her, 'Can I help with anything?'

She was so absorbed that she didn't hear me so I walked round and stood behind her. She was staring at a long order for groceries. It was written in a tiny old-fashioned hand, the lines and figures very close together. As I waited patiently behind her, Cook shook her head, put down the paper and went back to her work.

While she worked at the range I glanced down at the paper. It was just a list of quantities and goods and prices but it seemed horribly muddled. My old passion for figures and for order came back in a second and I became so absorbed in the paper I didn't notice Cook until it was too late and she was right by my side.

Oh my God, I'm for it now, I thought. But I quickly said, 'I'm sorry, I thought I might be able to help.'

I was certain Cook was about to give me a terrible telling-off but, almost in a whisper, she said, 'Can you make anything of it? I don't want to send it up to the housekeeper until I understand it in case she asks me about it. I don't want to look a fool.'

I did a quick calculation in my head and explained

where and how the list had got muddled. She gave me a stub of a pencil and asked me to correct the figures, which I did. Just then the housekeeper knocked and walked in. She was one of the very few in the house who didn't wait after knocking. We all froze and Cook was obliged to explain why we were scribbling rather than cooking.

'Kat is just helping me with one of the kitchen bills,' she said. She could hardly have said anything else as I'd been caught with pencil and paper in hand. Poor Cook looked very uncomfortable.

'Helping. Is she now,' said the housekeeper. 'Well, if it's a bill let me have it when you have both finished with it.'

And with that she turned and walked out.

Honestly, the airs and graces that woman gave herself would make you think she was married to the head of the family rather than employed by him. She had positively flounced out of the kitchen.

Secretly I was delighted by all this because I knew I had made a good job of adding up the figures and making sense of the bill and I'd been spotted doing it by the person who really mattered. Even Cook, who'd initially looked embarrassed, had a look of relief once the housekeeper had gone and I'd set out the figures on the back of the bill in a way she could understand.

Chapter 26

After my success with the bill I expected something, anything, to happen but of course nothing changed. The months passed uneventfully with only the usual below-stairs gossip to pass the time. My two friends, Nessa and Netta, were the main source of all my fun. It is amazing how young girls thrown together from very different backgrounds can sometimes hit it off wonderfully. In a big house, which was in many ways like a prison, friendships could be incredibly intense because servants often felt as if the whole world was against them. It's the old story I suppose of adversity making strange bedfellows.

Nessa was a tall, dark girl with a small rosebud mouth and very dark arching eyebrows of which she was very proud. She had intense black eyes and overall looked every inch the gypsy. She wasn't conventionally pretty but she had the loveliest hair. It was very thick and a sort of glossy raven black.

Girls were obsessed with their hair at that time – even servant girls – and hated ever to get it cut. I remember reading that girls at art schools in London were scandalising the city by cutting their hair into the newly fashionable bob and I was horrified. Why would they want to do that? Like Nessa I loved my hair and thought it was my most attractive feature even if most of the time it was tied up with a mass of pins under my cap.

Netta was much shorter than Nessa and extremely slim with brown hair and the sort of skin that burns in an instant. She had a mouth that seemed slightly too big for her face and she used to say, 'I've got far too many teeth. It's awful but I can't afford to have them out. Who will have me like this? I'm like a dangerous fish!'

She certainly had a wonderfully wide grin but it was part of her charm. She disliked her hair almost as much as her teeth.

'I'm so mousy and thin,' she would wail, 'and my hair is mousy and thin. Even my legs are mousy and thin!'

I listened to this most nights as we got ready for bed. I used to say to her, 'No it isn't thin at all. It's fine and delicate. All depends how you look at it.'

The three of us went into town now and then when we had the same Sunday off, as we did occasionally. We'd get the bus which groaned and rattled up and down the low Leicestershire hills and seemed to take an age to cover half a mile.

I remember we saw a cowboy film and it was one of those tremendously exciting things you never forget because none of us had ever seen a film before. I had never heard a radio let alone seen moving pictures. In fact I didn't really believe that moving pictures existed until I saw my first film. Before the great event I just couldn't imagine how it would look, but I could have watched that first film over and over again.

Decades later I watched an old black-and-white silent film of the kind I'd seen when young and it looked shaky and badly acted and frankly boring. But things were different in the 1920s and that film was the highlight of the decade for me. I have no idea now what it was called or who was in it but if I close my eyes I can see again the flickering pictures that straight away bring to mind that early thrill.

Chapter 27

At the house I gradually became aware of the habits and interests of the family because although we had so little contact with them we couldn't help but gossip about what they might or might not be doing. This was officially frowned on but what could anyone do to stop it? The housekeeper and butler made it clear that anyone caught gossiping would be in trouble but with so little else to amuse us even the risk of being sacked would not have been enough to stop us talking.

It was rumoured that the master – he was a baronet but we all referred to him as His Lordship – was obsessed with germs and terrified of becoming ill. Lots of people were funny about this sort of thing at the time because people still remembered the great flu epidemic of 1918–19 that killed millions across the word. Medicine was also a very hit-and-miss affair.

The result of His Lordship's terror of germs was that Cook was under strict instructions to ensure everything was really well cooked. That meant the roasts were almost burned to a cinder by the time she'd finished with them and ducks, geese and chickens were cooked till there was almost nothing left but crispy fat. This upset Cook but she had to do what she was told.

Vegetables were always boiled or roasted in those days so there was an idea that they were always safe. Jams and preserves were a different matter. We were not allowed to make them at all despite all the fruit produced in the kitchen garden. His Lordship was convinced that home-made jams and jellies were a fatal source of germs so jams and chutneys, pickles and preserves were all sent up by train from Fortnum and Mason in London, in special hampers.

His Lordship wore white gloves almost all the time and whenever he ordered books from London he would send them down to the kitchen still in their brown paper parcels so that Cook and I were the first to open them and risk the onslaught of those terrible germs. We were instructed to put the books in the oven for ten minutes to kill any germs. I had to supervise this and it was a nerve-wracking business because if you got it wrong the pages became brittle and fell apart in your hands and then there was hell to pay. So I was careful to check every minute or so that they were warmed up but not too hot. I'm sure it made absolutely no difference but it kept His Lordship happy. All the staff were forbidden ever to bring a library book into the house – even if we agreed to roast it first.

It shows how much in awe we were of the boss that we didn't just keep the books in the kitchen for a while and then send them back up without bothering to go through the oven business. How would he ever have known we hadn't left them in the oven for the required ten minutes? The truth is he would never have known, but no one ever thought of cheating like this out of the sheer terror of being found out.

In addition to his hygiene craze, His Lordship had a thing about pyjamas. He had dozens if not hundreds of pairs which were constantly being washed, much to the annoyance of the laundry maids. He absolutely insisted that his pyjamas be ironed and he insisted on two cleaned and ironed pairs being sent up every day.

His Lordship was also a great letter-writer, according at least to the footmen. I was told that he wrote constantly to *The Times* and *Country Life* and he was furious if his letters were not published. He also wrote regularly to *The Field* magazine. I thought this was a farming magazine until one of the footmen showed me a letter it had published from His Lordship.

'Go on, have a look,' said the footman, so I read it. The letter seemed a very angry, almost rude response to a letter that had been published the previous week. His Lordship called the other correspondent an incompetent and a charlatan and challenged him to a shooting match to prove who was right. I had no idea what this was all about so I said to the footman, 'Well, so what if His Lordship writes to say someone else doesn't know what he is talking about?'

'No, no, that's not the point,' said the footman. 'You don't get it, do you?'

'No, I don't,' I said.

'The person who wrote the letter His Lordship is attacking is also His Lordship! He wrote the first letter under a pseudonym and then wrote using his own name to ridicule his earlier letter. He thinks it's hilarious.'

Apparently the old man loved doing this and he was always writing letters to fishing magazines and country magazines, creating an argument and then creating two letter-writers who would fight it out in the pages of whichever journal it might be. In his letters to *The Times* he liked to suggest cures for baldness. The footman told me that His Lordship had written several to say that burnt toast mixed with water and then rubbed into the scalp was a sure-fire way to cure hairlessness.

The footman told me that he had to attend His Lordship whenever he had a letter-writing session. He always knew when the letters were likely to be mischievous because His Lordship would chuckle madly to himself as he wrote. He would also mutter and talk to himself while writing. The footman overheard him saying, 'You can write what you like to that magazine' – he meant *The Field* – 'because the staff are so stupid they will print anything!'

His Lordship was not always so lucky with *The Times* and they did not always fall for his pranks. When the footman was asked to tidy the desk one day he found a letter from the editor which said, 'Please do not bother to write again.' Underneath His Lordship had scrawled 'bloody impudence!'

His Lordship's other great project was the invention of a bag designed to catch horse droppings. Now, by this time horses were disappearing rapidly; they were hardly used anywhere except on farms and here and there by the odd eccentric, but His Lordship was convinced the fashion for motor vehicles would come to an end and we'd all be driving around in carriages again.

The footman showed me a note about the horse-dung bag that had been written by His Lordship:

> The problem with horses is the rather unseemly business of defecation. They defecate whenever they feel like it and this frequently occurs in the very sight of delicate females who are obliged to ride behind the horse at precisely the worst possible position. My patented device will ensure that when the horse obeys its natural instincts the specially constructed device will catch the offending droppings in such a way that any ladies present will remain unaware that anything untoward is happening.

The idea was drummed into me too when, using more or less the same words, His Lordship described his invention to all the staff one Sunday morning after the usual Bible reading in the hall. You might have thought the staff would hate this but they enjoyed it far more than the Bible reading. The old man's eccentricity was the best thing about him so far as the servants were concerned.

Chapter 28

After my success with the muddled kitchen bill I carried on with my work and then after I'd been at the house for more than five years and had begun to think nothing would ever change, something curious happened. I was busy chopping vegetables in the kitchen when the door opened and instead of a footman waiting to carry dishes upstairs it was the hall boy. He looked around and caught Cook's eye.

'Mrs Martin wants Kat,' he said. Mrs Martin was the housekeeper.

I looked at the boy and I looked at Cook. She nodded very gravely at me so I carefully cleaned my hands and ran along the corridor to the housekeeper's room. This was where all the household accounts were done and, more importantly, where they were stored. In fact the account books went back more than half a century because as the old ledgers were filled up they were stored carefully in a long, glass-fronted mahogany cabinet that went from floor to ceiling.

The housekeeper's room was where the butler and senior footman had lunch, waited on hand and foot by the junior staff. To me it seemed a very beautiful room with prints of the estate as it had been in previous centuries hanging on the wall and a pretty, light green wallpaper with a delicate leaf pattern that looked as good as anything upstairs.

The housekeeper's room was actually more like a small flat and she had her own bedroom there as well as the sitting room that doubled as her office. It also had an unusually big fireplace – it seemed far too big for the room, but when I mentioned this to Nessa she said, 'All that pen work – doesn't generate any heat does it. Not like us rushing about and warm all the time. Poor old dear would freeze her scribbling finger without a huge fire!'

I straightened my cap when I reached the door and then knocked. The housekeeper shouted to come in and in I went. She was sitting at her work table and smiled at me, which was very unusual.

'Kat,' she said. 'I remember you were good at sorting out Cook's bill from the stores.'

I thought, Good heavens, you have a tremendous memory – that was years ago!

Then she said, 'I wonder if you would tell me what you think of this.'

'Yes,' I replied.

I was so taken aback that I stayed rooted to the spot staring stupidly at her.

'Well, come on then,' she said, and she waved me around to her side of the table.

I looked down at a series of columns, long, complicated lists of figures with corrections and bits of working-out all over the place as well as dozens of loose bills and invoices. Next to the papers was a huge account book into which I think the housekeeper was hoping to copy the figures for various things once she had made sense of them.

I started going down the columns and they were in a terrible mess but I was sure I could make sense of them.

'Get yourself that chair,' said the housekeeper, pointing to one over against the wall.

I dragged the chair across and sat down. At first the figures danced in front of my eyes and it was difficult to see where the muddle had started and where it might end. I was amazed that the housekeeper, whose main job this was, had allowed things to get to this stage, but as in all walks of life there are always some people who get jobs they really shouldn't get, either because they know the right people or because it's Buggins's turn. That's not really being fair on the housekeeper in this case because she was, I think, very good at the other parts of her job – she was excellent at keeping track of linen, preserves, storage and so on. But I think her weak point was the figures. Luckily for her and for me I didn't have to look at figures for long before they sort of arranged themselves into patterns in front of my eyes that made complete sense.

However, this was a little awkward at first because as I sat there I felt I was on trial with the great ledger in front of me and Mrs Martin right by my shoulder watching my every move. It was like the worst sort of exam where you are watched at every turn.

Anyway, my luck held and eventually I asked for a separate piece of paper and did a few simple sums and calculations and then asked if I could make a few changes to the list of figures already entered in the ledger.

The housekeeper didn't answer so I looked carefully up at her. She was staring carefully at the paper and even a little suspiciously as if I might at any minute do something that would get her into terrible trouble. It was as if she was afraid she was about to be taken in by a confidence trickster! Her eyes narrowed a bit and she said, 'Go on then, but be careful. Her Ladyship will look at this.'

I got back to my work and with a reordering of the figures on the paper and a few crossings-out here and there, the month's accounts began to add up.

I explained what I'd done to the housekeeper in as meek and mild a way as I could because I could see she was baffled by what I was doing. If there was the least sense I was talking down to her she'd have taken against me and made my life very difficult, so I was careful to explain in such a way that it seemed as if someone else had come in and jumbled things up and only the house-keeper and I had the brains to sort them out.

At the end of half an hour I was able to breathe a sigh of relief when she said, 'You have been helpful. You may go now.'

'Yes ma'am,' I said and did a little curtsey.

'And Kat,' she said as I reached the door.

'Yes ma'am?'

'Thank you.'

And she smiled at me.

Now in service a big, friendly smile from your superior was a very rare thing indeed.

I was delighted with myself after this. I walked back to the kitchen feeling very cocky and smiling to myself – and you can hardly blame me because amid the endless humdrum of life below stairs this sort of thing very rarely happened. In fact I'd say that it was unheard of. My success, small as it was, had a good effect in the long term but a bad effect in the short term.

'What was that all about?' Cook demanded as soon as I got back to the kitchen.

'Mrs Martin had got in a muddle with the accounts and asked me if I could help a bit,' I said

I tried to make it sound as if I'd done a very small thing indeed but another bit of me thought, Why should I keep quiet about helping someone much older and more experienced than me? Just because we were all supposed to be permanently humble, was I to pretend that I hadn't done anything at all? But given what was to happen, I probably should have lied and said the housekeeper wanted me for something trivial.

I explained in a bit more detail that the accounts had needed some work but as I spoke I noticed a shift in the way Cook looked at me. For the rest of that day she hardly said a word to me.

Wasn't that typical, I thought. Cook had started the whole thing off by asking me about her list of figures and now I was in trouble for looking at someone else's list of figures!

A friend of mine once said that domestics are all extremes. They either get on really well or they are constantly at each other's throats. It is certainly true in my experience that resentments sometimes simmered for years. I knew two maids, for example, who hated each other because their mothers, who had worked in the same house as the daughters, disliked each other – it was like a feud that went on for generations and long after everyone had forgotten the original cause of the trouble.

Well, after that day with the housekeeper, Cook, who had always been nice enough to me, became very bad-tempered and sullen. I knew straight away why. She thought I was getting above myself or was getting favourable treatment, which is something servants were obsessed about. It was impossible to have it out with her. It would have made no difference if I'd said, 'I just helped Mrs Martin. I haven't been having tea and muffins with her.' Even if I'd been able to say that or something like it, Cook would not have believed me. In her eyes she'd been shown up – humiliated I mean – by an underling.

So things got slowly worse for me after that, even though the housekeeper didn't ask me again to help with anything and never showed in any way that I was being given special treatment. The whole thing was ridiculous but typical of the feuds that sometimes erupted for very little reason below stairs.

I was made to do the worst tasks that the scullery maid should really have done and Cook even stopped asking me to run errands to the gardener or the gardener's boy, almost as if she couldn't bear to let me out of her sight in case someone asked me to do something of which she disapproved.

Imagine the silence all the long day in that gloomy, high-ceilinged kitchen, with work to be done hour after hour and not a word out of the only person in the room with you.

I remember weeks passed after Cook took against me. Without a word out of her the kitchen became a silent place. It was awful. One day as winter came on I remember looking out the tall kitchen windows and seeing the rain pouring down across the yard and the distant trees and park. For miles in every direction there were only the dripping trees and an occasional distant car or horse and cart to remind me that something would have to change to get me out of this.

Time passed and Cook tended to find fault more and more. She began speaking to me again but never in a friendly tone.

One morning almost a year later when I was sure she must have started to get over what had happened I was laying out the boards and various knives and spoons when she rushed across and pushed me away from the big table.

'No, not like that,' she said in a furious voice. 'How many times do I have to tell you that you need to leave more space for me? More space is what I need. Not everything cluttered together as you have it.'

I felt very tearful all of a sudden as I had taken so much care to do everything just as she wanted it so as not to provoke her and in some hope that she would go back to her old friendly ways. But the housekeeper business was always on her mind.

I began to hate Cook, the job, the house and even Leicestershire. I began not sleeping well and several times dreamed I was being given a terrible telling-off by Cook. In one dream she threw knives and plates at me and I could feel them showering down on me like a rain of sharp cutting pieces and when I looked at my hands they were covered in blood. I woke up with a terrible start and though I realised it had only been a dream the terror took a long time to pass. I couldn't get back to sleep. I remember going out and along the narrow, dark corridor outside our room to the nearest window and looking across the park and thinking that even the bloody pheasants were better off – they only got shot at in the shooting season and not the whole bloody time like me!

All my efforts to be as quiet and obedient as possible were failing so I began to think the only solution was to find another job. Leaving was the only power the servant had in those days, but it was a real power because, as I've said, there were always lots of jobs going.

I began looking in the local newspaper. There would often be a paper in the servants' hall and when it looked a bit knocked about I knew it would be OK for me to take it because the top servants would already have seen it. If it was still smooth and looked unread I would never touch it. The family only ever read the national papers, never the local one.

I was all at sea of course with the idea of starting again somewhere new. I had liked the big Leicestershire house and the village where all the locals tipped their hats to me and I had Netta and Nessa always to talk to. I liked it all except for the fact that Cook had turned against me. Often I wondered how anyone could hold a grudge for so long. But then I remembered those maids who had continued a feud from one generation to the next.

I had no desire at all to get back to London because although I'd never found much to do in the country-side, I enjoyed the peace and quiet – when you've had nothing but crowded rooms and smelly streets, a few fields can be a bit of a tonic and they certainly were for me; but it was such a strain working in that kitchen for someone who clearly no longer liked me.

At last the newspaper came up trumps and I found a position that looked as if it might be suitable. Most of the ads in the paper were for ladies' maids and kitchen maids and housemaids so there was plenty to choose from. The maid's position I decided to apply for was in a house about five miles away so I thought to myself, If I get an interview I can easily walk there and back on my day off.

Who would think of walking ten miles in a day to apply for a job today? Very few I suspect, but no one thought anything of such things in the 1930s. I wrote to the address given and waited, and waited. This would have been about 1934. I remember thinking that if and when a letter did arrive I would have to be careful that I got to it quickly. I was terrified Cook would see it and ask what was in it as I never normally received letters. Some of the other staff received mail now and then and anything for us was left on a table in the servants' hall in the morning – there were still three or four postal deliveries a day back then so I had to keep dashing out of the kitchen to make sure that if a letter had arrived as few other people as possible saw it before I was able to collect it.

Nessa and Netta wondered why my parents didn't write to me but the truth is they could hardly write at all and such a thing would never have occurred to them.

At last, just when I began to think I would need to start looking in the newspaper again, I saw my name on a cream envelope all alone on the big old table. I grabbed it and stuffed it down the front of my blue dress without even thinking about opening it. It wasn't till ten o'clock that evening that I was able to steal up to my room and open it. For some silly reason I thought they might have offered me the job there and then as had been the case before; but I was close enough for an interview and they would have known that, of course.

I quickly realised that even if I got through the interview, there was another hurdle to be negotiated. I would have to get a reference and though the housekeeper would provide it she would be bound to ask Cook about me. I didn't know at this stage that in fact it was not always necessary to have a reference because it was common knowledge that employers would occasionally give a member of staff a bad reference to stop them leaving. So increasingly new employers relied on how you were in the interview.

At least now there was a chance I might escape Cook's bitter little stares and her horrible way of saying, 'You need to mend your ways Kathleen or you'll never get anywhere.' Or she'd say now and then, 'You really are bloody useless,' or she'd wander round muttering, 'Hopeless, hopeless,' under her breath without appearing to be referring to anyone.

So I replied to the housekeeper at the other house and can still remember dashing down the drive very early one morning before starting work to post my letter saying I would come for the interview.

Letters written by members of the family were taken to the post by the hall boy but we staff had to take our own letters down the drive and into the village which was about half a mile away. I ran like the wind knowing that if I was a second later than usual in the kitchen, Cook would be even grumpier than usual.

In my reply I had said only two things beyond giving the basic details of who I was and what I had been doing. I said I would come for an interview and I asked if I could do so on the second or last Sunday of the month.

You'd think that with all this toing and froing of letters that it would take forever to sort things out but don't forget that letters arrived more quickly then – in London you could still post a letter in the morning and it would be delivered that evening if the recipient was also in London.

Another week passed with me dashing in and out of the servants' hall whenever Cook went to the lavatory or was called up to see the housekeeper. I was desperate for another letter telling me that Sunday was an acceptable day and at what time I should present myself.

Looking back I don't know why it didn't occur to me that Cook would be delighted to hear I wanted to leave as she'd taken so badly against me. But I was young and silly and didn't always think straight then. I thought that anything I wanted to do would inevitably enrage her and in all the months since my visit to the housekeeper to help with the figures I'd never been asked to help with the accounts again. I'd secretly thought I might become the housekeeper's assistant so when all went quiet and I was once again forgotten in my steamy hot corner of the kitchen I was hugely disappointed.

The little door that had briefly opened into a brighter future seemed to have closed.

But at last another letter came, the date for my interview was agreed and when the Sunday came round I set off on the five-mile trudge to what I hoped might eventually be my new place of work.

Chapter 29

On most of my days off I had little to do unless Nessa and I went into town, which we often did to stare at the boys – if there were any to stare at – and see a film in the picture house or just have a cup of tea. Now my next Sunday off suddenly had a more serious purpose. It was my chance to move somewhere else and start again, even though I would still be a blooming kitchen maid.

I remember that walk so well. It was late summer and very still and hot. The stitching had burst on my old coat but I'd checked it the night before and fixed it as well as I could, as well as the lining which had been hanging down at the back. I thought I mustn't look too much of a scruff. It was a cheap old coat but I liked it because I thought it showed off my figure!

A car passed me after about half a mile and I looked back to see it go and the driver squeezed his hooter to acknowledge me and lifted his hand. I loved watching cars and this was a beauty. I listened as its drone became more distant and then vanished and all around I could hear only the sound of birdsong and a distant barking dog.

The narrow road wound on but there wasn't much of a view a great deal of the time because the hedge-rows were thick with trees, mostly elms I think, which were everywhere then. A girl on a lonely road in the 1930s was not such an unusual sight as it would have been in later years and several farm workers waved to me from the fields as I went by and passed a place now and then where there were gaps in the hedge or a gate. But as I padded along I thought how little I knew about the countryside and how different it was from London.

There were as many odd things about the country-side as there were about the town. For example, I remembered how Nessa had been upset one day when the hall boy teased her and said, 'Yer bed's made out of elm planks.' Why on earth would that upset her? I wondered, and so I asked.

'Elms are for coffins,' she replied. 'It's terrible bad luck.' She was a very superstitious girl in many ways – in fact all the country girls I had met in the house seemed to me to be well behind us city girls in almost everything. They really believed for example in ghosts and Netta absolutely insisted she had seen at least two. But that business with the elm wood really took the biscuit.

Nessa had quoted a little rhyme to me: 'Elm hateth man, And waiteth.'

She said her father used to walk about the place shouting at the elms, 'I'm not ready for you yet!'

These and other thoughts filled my mind as I walked along and gradually grew hotter and hotter from walking in my thick coat. I had plenty of time so I decided to sit for a while by a stone gate. Nothing worse than arriving in a muck sweat!

And do you know, for almost ten minutes nothing came along the road and there was hardly a sound except for the birds.

I think the period before the Second World War was the last time when you could do that in England without cars and lorries and people rushing by you every minute or so.

After I'd cooled down I set off again and though I was used to walking my feet began to hurt. I thought, This is bloody marvellous – what will they think of me all in a sweat and hobbling and covered in flies. The flies, great clouds of them, had suddenly appeared from nowhere. There were no insecticides on the farms and with cattle, sheep and horse dung piled up at the sides of fields, insects were a huge problem.

I saw a string of massive farm horses ambling towards me and I thought, In London the boys could have made a fortune here, because when those horses produced dung they produced it by the hundredweight!

At last I could see the big brick house ahead of me. It had an enormous garden all round it, but hardly the great park and the long drive I was used to. The house couldn't be missed because suddenly the hedges and big trees came to an end and an ancient red brick wall about five feet high appeared. Now this wall was a marvel which I've never forgotten. Instead of being straight like any other wall you've ever seen it was like a snake! Looked at from above it would have been like a squiggly line and it was hundreds of yards long and must have cost a fortune because it would have taken twice as many bricks and man hours to build as a straight wall.

But that was just the first oddity about a house that came to seem very odd indeed to me, and in so many ways.

Past the serpentine wall I found a double gate which was rusted and on one side half off its hinges. I nipped through and walked slightly uneasily up the short drive, which, with hardly any gravel, was more of an overgrown lane, until I reached the front of the house.

I stood still, wondering where I should go to find the servants' entrance when out of the corner of my eye I noticed an old man standing just a few feet from me. I hadn't seen him as I'd walked up but how I'd missed him till I was almost under his nose I can't imagine.

'Who are you?' he said. He was neither friendly nor unfriendly. He wore torn trousers and a camel-coloured coat with torn pockets. He was pushing a pram filled with leaves and sticks.

'I've come to see Mrs Charlton, the housekeeper,' I blurted out.

'I see,' he said. 'Well you need to go round that way and you'll find a door open at the side of the house. Go in there and someone will see you.'

With that he smiled and showed teeth as brown as old tobacco.

I smiled back, turned and left him.

Must be the gardener, I thought.

I found the door just where he said it would be. It was half open so I peeped in. I saw that the door led straight into the kitchen, which was all bustle.

So I stood like an idiot on the threshold completely unsure what to do next. The two girls I could see were absorbed in something and I was reluctant to disturb them, but I noticed they were talking to each other and in an easy, friendly sort of way. I sensed immediately that the atmosphere in this kitchen was far better than that back at the big house; and that maybe the cook was more human, not riddled with jealousy. Suddenly one of the two girls caught sight of me and ran over.

'You're the new maid, aren't you?' she said.

'I don't know,' I said. 'Maybe. I have to see the housekeeper first.'

'Oh Mrs Charlton, you'll like her. Everybody does. Come with me.'

Well I've never felt as instantly welcome as I did in the housekeeper's room. Mrs Charlton was friendlier than I could ever have hoped, so much so that when she asked me why I wanted to move I was completely open and told her about the incident with the accounts. I saw her take note of that and I thought, 'Oh no, she will think I'm a troublemaker. But then she said, 'That's really useful. You can help me with the accounts and the bills here which will stand you in good stead if you ever want to move later on and become a housekeeper yourself.'

Mrs Charlton loved the idea that she would have some help if she needed it and she seemed delighted when I confessed that my ambition was to be a housekeeper.

'Well we must help you all we can,' she said. 'Would you like to start work next month?'

I walked the five miles back to the old house in a daydream of delight. I felt that at last I might have the chance to get on in life. So many visions appeared to me of what the future might hold – more money and interesting work and escape from the drudgery of the kitchen.

Most people in service felt that fate had dealt them a pretty miserable hand. They might go from junior housemaid to senior housemaid or from hall boy to butler but it was rare to go from kitchen maid to housekeeper. Yet that was still my plan – and I needed a bit of luck to do it. Perhaps with these new friendly people my luck really was beginning to turn.

Back at the big house I could hardly wait to hand my notice in. I told Cook my news straight away. There was no reaction but she was slightly nicer to me during my last few weeks, as if a great burden had been lifted from her. Mrs Martin, the housekeeper, said she'd miss me and that was the end of that. No one ever tried to keep a servant, in my experience, by offering higher wages or more time off because that might make them think they were anything other than completely dispensable. If they felt that, they might start getting above themselves.

Nessa and Netta cried when I told them I was leaving because we were friends and girls always cried then – even I cried, but it made us all feel much better. I wasn't really upset because I thought we'd still be able see each other for our trips into town because five miles was not such a long way.

A month later I packed my bag and left it in the servants' hall to be sent on, kissed the girls goodbye, was ignored by Cook, and set off for my new home.

Chapter 30

The new house was so refreshing after the bitterness of below stairs in the old place. There seemed to be a much lighter atmosphere, partly I think because there were far fewer staff and partly because it didn't have the old stuck-in-the-mud traditions of a house on a big estate. The gentleman we worked for, Mr Barker, was a lawyer and a very eccentric one at that. But his eccentricities reduced the level of formality in the house rather than increased it.

On my first day, the housekeeper came to see me in the kitchen and reminded me of our earlier interview.

'You know you will have to become a cook before you can become a housekeeper, don't you?' she said.

'Yes,' I replied. 'I've kept up my own recipe book and noted down all the methods and dishes. I think I could be cook because I've learned the ropes so thoroughly. I'm well organised and am used to working in a very big kitchen.'

I'd never made such a long speech in my life but I was fed up feeling the underdog and bowing and scraping to everyone so I put a bit of vim into it!

Mrs Charlton smiled and said she thought we would get on.

The first few weeks in the new job were difficult because though everyone was friendly there were different ways of doing things and they took some getting used to.

After about a month Mrs Charlton called me to her room.

'Right,' she said. 'You have passed through your probation period and I want to give you a little test. I need some help now and then and I remember what you said about being good at figures so I'm going to give you something to do that's very different from the sort of thing we'd normally expect a kitchen maid to do.'

She left the room and came back in a short while with a pile of bills. Some were torn, some were in terrible handwriting and some listed a great many items. They were in a tremendous muddle. Just bundles all heaped together.

'I'll give you an hour to sort these out and add them up so they make sense. I want the total for the week for the butcher, the grocer and the others, and then I want the figures added up for the month and the year. I want the lists to be accurate – I need kitchen cleaning stuffs in one column, hardware in another, the grocer's bill separate from the greengrocer and the coal merchant and so on. Only make a sundries list where they are very small, individual items that don't fit anywhere else. Don't do any of the working-out in the book. I will give you a piece of paper and we can transfer the list when you have finished if all the figures make sense.'

Well here I was on trial all over again! My confidence momentarily left me. I sat looking through the enormous pile of scruffy bits of paper and then back and forth to my blank sheet. I was frozen. I looked at the big clock and realised that five minutes had already passed and that seemed to light a fire under my bottom.

I started work. First I sorted the bills into piles – there were so many of them! – then I did a simple bit of arithmetic to find a total for each pile, but I split them according to date so each list represented one week and did this for each of the headings the housekeeper had mentioned. When I'd finished I made a total for all the weeks covered and then the months. Everything was lined up in such a way that the cost of every single item from vegetables, tea and meat to new cups, linen and saucepans could easily be seen. The greatest difficulty had not been the figures themselves but the indecipherable scrawl in which many of the bills were written. Tradesmen were often not good at writing and even when they were, they often wrote their bills out in such a way that you might make a mistake in their favour. If doctors had a reputation for illegible handwriting tradesmen in my experience were far worse.

Working out the bills for a few groceries probably sounds easy for anyone who has spent a long time at senior school, but I knew from my own experience that many servant girls couldn't add up if their lives depended on it. Even by the 1940s many could still barely read or write. A girl might be wonderful at practical tasks round the house either as a kitchen maid or general maid but ask her to do a simple sum and it would be as if she were suddenly three years old again. I was so lucky that I had enjoyed a little more education.

The housekeeper, Mrs Charlton, was soon back in the room. She looked gravely over my figures, running her pencil up and down the lines. I held my breath, thinking, Please, please, don't let me have made a mistake!

Moments passed and then she looked up and smiled at me. A real and genuine smile.

'Well that's very good. Off you go now and we'll talk more about this later on.'

Chapter 31

Let me describe the house and the grounds, which were unusual. The house was on the edge of the village and it was far bigger than the little cottages along the curving village high street. But I don't think it had ever been what used to be called a gentleman's house – meaning that it was not designed to be run as a large household with numerous rooms for staff and several staircases and so on.

It was not what you would call a grand house. It was really just a sort of big old farmhouse that had at some stage been added to, so it had two wings tacked on, like an E without the middle bit. One of these wings had a basement and cellar though the main, older part of the house did not. The servants worked and lived in one of the Victorian wings which had bigger windows than the old part of the house and much higher ceilings so it was an odd set-up because superficially the servants had the best of it – the main house had low ceilings and a number of really quite small rooms that led off each other in awkward ways but the lawyer hated the idea of changing anything, or at least that's what the house-keeper told me.

The grounds were unusual too in the sense that there wasn't much land immediately attached to the house but Mr Barker owned other small plots beyond the village and other nearby villages. In one case he owned a wood in the middle of a huge field owned by someone else.

Around the house there were probably a couple of acres at most. Here Mr Barker kept several peacocks that howled mournfully day and night – several maids had left over the years because they couldn't stand the wailing, but it never bothered me much. There were also two donkeys in a small paddock bounded by an overgrown hedge. There was a gap in the hedge and through it every morning the donkeys came up to the house to stare gloomily through the kitchen window until they were shooed away or given a carrot. Either way they stayed for half an hour and then wandered off back through the gap in the hedge to their field. Mr Barker also kept a pig that he regularly talked to and fed personally.

I remember my first day in my room at the top of the stairs in the Victorian wing. And here was another oddity. To get to my room I had to go up a staircase built on the outside of the end of the wing. It was stone and completely open to the elements. On each landing of the three storeys the stone staircase had a door into the house.

My room was right at the top and I remember countless times in winter how I'd run out of the downstairs door from the kitchen into the yard and then up the stone staircase with the rain soaking me and the wind howling round my ears every step of the way.

I had a bedroom on my own now and the house-maids – two of them – shared the next room along the corridor. I was the only kitchen maid. When I tell people that in addition to my uniform I had two dresses, a coat and two pairs of shoes and these were the things I put in my little cupboard I get looks of horror. Is that all you had? people ask. Well, it *was* all I had. I didn't have a picture of my parents or friends or of my brothers because no one had ever taken a photo of them. You never saw photographers down Paddington way though there were expensive picture shops in the West End. But we'd never go there.

No one in service felt bad about having few possessions then because we, I mean servants in general, were all in the same boat – none of the maids I knew had much. Even when I became a housekeeper I never owned much in the way of orna-ments or pictures. I eventually bought some second-hand furniture but that was only when I was no longer in service. I think the rich often had a worse time of it in this respect because if they fell on hard times their poverty showed up more – they'd 'come down', as people used to say. They'd had all those lovely things and when they had to sell them, when the auctioneers came in as they did increasingly in the 1950s, it was deeply upsetting. Servants had so much less to lose.

Chapter 32

My new job was wonderfully different from the old one. No one in the new house minded a bit that I helped the housekeeper now and then as well as worked in the kitchen because it had been made clear to Cook at the outset that I might have other duties. Admittedly this was a very unusual arrangement – in fact I would say it was unique in service and I think it was only really possible because the housekeeper was a bit of a lazybones and liked me to add up and keep her account books to save her the trouble. Partly also of course this was a smaller house without all the ancient rules and regulations of a more feudal place.

So I was much happier here and felt I might soon attain my ambition of carrying the housekeeper's bunch of keys.

I benefitted in other ways from the oddities of the house and the eccentricity of its owner, which I discovered a few weeks after starting work.

Mr Barker, the lawyer, was a very strange man. Everyone said so. In fact they said it again and again and you heard it all over the surrounding villages, but most people thought he was quite harmless. I was amazed he was able to earn a living at all, but he was really two men. He was sane enough when he went to London on the train to hear a criminal case – he was apparently a well-known barrister – but he allowed his oddities their fullest expression at home.

He used to ask for a particular maid now and then to clean his room in the afternoon. In all houses it was standard for the rooms to be cleaned in the morning after or during the family breakfast, so this on its own was strange enough. But it was common knowledge that Mr Barker asked for her because she was pretty and very young, definitely not more than fifteen I think. He would stay in his bedroom while she cleaned and then he would say, 'Would you mind cleaning the tops of the pictures?' He had a small set of steps in his bedroom and she used these to reach the pictures. She knew perfectly well why he was asking her to clean the picture tops. It was so he could look at her legs.

'Every time I catch his eye out of the corner of my eye,' the maid told me, 'he is staring like mad at my bottom half.' But she didn't mind, she said, because at the end of every one of these sessions he would give her a shilling or half a crown before patting her on the bottom and sending her on her way.

'He's a harmless old thing,' she would say, 'and he pays good money.'

Another of his oddities was that he collected samplers. I had no idea what a sampler was until someone showed me one. It's a small bit of embroidery usually commemorating some event or other or it might have the name of the girl who worked it and the date embroidered in a pattern of flowers. Mr Barker had dozens of samplers going back to the 1600s and some were very beautiful.

They were all over the walls of one of the smaller rooms where he liked to sit and read. I got to see this room and many others in the main part of the house despite being just a kitchen maid. In a big, aristocratic house I would never have left the kitchen. But Mr Barker, with his eccentric ways, would call certain maids up by name to see him now and then. It should always have been the butler really who waited on him but his legs were not as attractive as the maids'!

I lost count of the number of times I would be in the kitchen and someone would call down, 'Kat, he wants you in the sitting room.' It was usually either me or the pretty housemaid, never the cook or the other maid. He had regular meetings with the housekeeper but they were formal and to discuss running costs and he came down rather than calling her up.

When he called for me I never knew what it might be about. Sometimes, though rarely, it was just for a chat. I think he liked the company of people who were not from his class. I think he felt more at ease with us because we were not like his clients down in London – from the rougher end of things.

But there was a shock in store for me. At my very first meeting with him I realised I had met him already. He was the man in the torn coat in the drive with the pram full of leaves, the ragged clothes and the terrible brown teeth!

My second meeting with him went like this.

'You're Kathleen, aren't you? How do you like the kitchen? And what about Cook? Do you get on?'

'We do sir, thank you,' I replied.

'Now, you're not a local girl, are you? I'd say London from your accent.'

'That's right sir. Paddington.'

'Oh Paddington. I know it well. Tremendous place. Full of life. I remember prosecuting the Simpson brothers. They were from Paddington. A most entertaining pair. Highly intelligent.'

'Yes sir,' I said, thinking how this was a funny old carry-on. What was he getting at? Well, he wasn't getting at anything; he just liked to talk and always in little short bursts. Over the years I was to have many similar meetings.

But Mr Barker was also interested in his servants or at least that's how it seemed. For example, he said to me quite early on, 'I hear you want to be housekeeper.'

'I do sir,' I replied. 'More than anything.'

'Why?'

Now that was an odd question because, apart from enjoying keeping the records and feeling that as housekeeper I would have some status, I really did not have a good explanation.

'I'd like to get on, sir,' I said. 'It pays a little more and I love working with arithmetic and accounts.'

'Well, would you be prepared to do anything to get such a job? Would you do anything I asked?'

Now this was an odd line to take and I hadn't really a clue what he was getting at, although I was to find out!

I must have looked very awkward because rather than wait for an answer he said: 'Very good, very good. We'll talk about that later and we'll see what we can do.'

I turned to leave the room and just as I reached the door he said, 'Before you go, I wonder, would you mind stepping up on that little table for a moment?'

I hesitated for a moment, unsure if I had misheard him, but in those days you did what your employer told you to do. If he'd told me to jump out the window I probably would have done it.

I felt myself turning horribly red as I climbed up first on a chair and then on to a very solid low square table. I stood feeling very foolish.

'Would you mind facing the window?' he asked.

I turned a little till I was where he said I should be and then I felt his hand on the backs of my calves. He squeezed gently and stroked them a bit, one hand on each calf. Then he ran his hand up till it was just above my knee. I could feel him caressing the front of my thigh.

He stopped and there was a pause. I dared not look round.

'Thank you,' he said. 'That will be all. You may go now.'

I climbed down thinking, this is very odd. What is it about older men? First I had to put up with Cackles as a child and now this. I knew this vaguely had to do with sex but what could I do? I liked the rest of the job and no one ever in my experience told an employer he could not do something. I felt rather ashamed later on especially as I'd have punched someone from my own class if they'd try to do the same thing.

I realised that this was the same sort of thing he did with the pretty housemaid. I don't think he had any other, proper relationships with women – or men for that matter. Certainly he didn't have a girlfriend and he was not married so I supposed that was how he coped.

In those days we all thought all older men were a bit dotty when it came to young women and girls. Mr Barker's leg stroking wasn't very nice but when, like the housemaid, I found he was paying me each time he made me stand on the table I decided it wouldn't be that difficult to put up with it.

Chapter 33

I was to stay with Mr Barker until his death so it can't have been all bad. After three years I was still helping Mrs Charlton with the accounts but I was doing it more often and I was also asked to go up to see Mr Barker once a fortnight to explain the expenditure and ask for money to pay the tradesmen – and of course to stand on the table. Mrs Charlton, the housekeeper, who should have been doing all the accounts work, loved it because she was getting on a bit and had bad arthritis and a number of other ailments about which she loved to complain.

'Kat, you're a wonder,' she used to say. 'Saving my legs. Are you sure you don't mind?'

Imagine that. Me being asked if I minded! Of course I didn't. I think I must have been the only kitchen maid in the country who was allowed such responsibility.

Sometimes as I explained the accounts to Mr Barker I would find he was just staring at me and not listening to a word I said. He never queried the sums of money and I think and hope he was rather impressed by how meticulous I was.

Then after about five years in the new house things began to change and they changed very quickly. Cook decided to leave and I simply took over where she left off but without being told in any formal way that I had been appointed cook. All the time I expected a real cook to be given the job but it didn't happen and one day the housekeeper said, 'Mr Barker is quite happy so just carry on as you are.'

So instead of appointing a new cook they appointed a new kitchen maid, a girl from the village who hardly opened her mouth in the first six months she worked with me. She was called Polly but everyone called her Poppet for some reason. She was very sweet and far too gentle ever to get anywhere.

'Come on, Poppet, look sharp and you'll be cook in no time,' I used to say.

'I don't think I could do it, Mrs Clifford,' she'd say. 'No, it would wallop me for certain.'

'Of course it wouldn't,' I said.

'No I don't think so.'

She had such an air of defeat about her right from the start. It was sad. When she was first brought down to the kitchen she did a little curtsey to me and to the housekeeper who looked up to heaven as if to say, 'What kind of an idiot is this!' because curtseying had gone out thirty years earlier.

But Poppet wasn't an idiot at all just very shy and very unsure of herself. She quickly learned the ropes and had everything laid out for me every morning in plenty of time. I noticed too that she cleaned everything brilliantly, especially the big pans which were the devil to make shine.

But it was as if she didn't *want* to have a personality. She had absolutely no get-up-and-go, as we used to say. I used to worry because if any and every boy in the village had walked up to Poppet and said, 'Lift up your skirts for a minute,' she'd have done it without a murmur. Talk about an innocent! She was the sort of girl who would get pregnant and then say, 'How did that happen?'

Chapter 34

I knew many recipes off by heart by now although I was never going to be a great chef. In my experience people in England before the 1960s hardly ever ate anything fancy – 'fancy' mostly meant foreign and the distrust of foreigners and anything foreign in England after the First World War would have to be experienced to be believed.

The most exotic thing I ever cooked for Mr Barker was oxtail soup with pepper, beef Wellington and fish in a caper sauce. Capers seemed the height of exotic cooking then. Mr Barker was highly suspicious about eating anything he hadn't eaten before, so he refused to eat anything new. When I once made the mistake of asking him if he would like a French stew – I suggested boeuf bourguignon – he said, 'No, Kat. If I want foreign slops I can get them in Fleet Street when I'm down in London. Let's just have good ordinary English food made with ordinary good plain ingredients.'

But if he was plain and simple about his food he was not plain and simple about much else.

The business of touching the maids' legs would have marked Mr Barker out as eccentric, but that was only the start of it.

Over the years I worked for him he went from being eccentric to completely mad. I think he must have had some sort of slow-acting mental illness, a kind of dementia that started early.

Some days he came down very early to see me. There was nothing odd about this as he came down pretty regularly. In most households it was the mistress who came down, but we didn't have a mistress.

I suppose he could have given his instructions to the housekeeper or the butler, who would then come and tell me. But he never did anything the way other people did it. Instead he would come down to the kitchen and very politely ask if I could cook something extra as he had a friend coming or because he just fancied something different.

But here was a great peculiarity. Each time he told me a friend or a group of friends were coming to dinner I would cook enough and make sure that two or three places were laid at the table. I would always make a special effort and the maid would take the food up or the butler would if Mr Barker told us that he wanted him.

Then each and every time the same report would come back to me. No guests ever turned up. Mr Barker ate on his own. Below stairs we were convinced not that his friends always failed to arrive because of some mishap or change of mind but that they simply didn't exist; or, if they did, they had never been invited in the first place.

Then gradually things began to get worse.

First the pretty maid – the maid he was really after – asked if she could be excused from going upstairs ever. Instead of just feeling her legs he had apparently asked her to do something she couldn't even describe to the housekeeper or me because she was so embarrassed.

I had noticed an even more absent air than usual when I went through the accounts with him and since I'd become cook he gradually stopped asking me to climb up on the table. Instead he would sit next to me and absent-mindedly run his hand up and down my leg.

People will think I was a terrible tart for allowing this but I found it difficult to make a fuss largely because I was making a lot of money from him and I didn't want to lose my job now that the job of house-keeper really was in sight.

The more I let him touch me the more he paid as I left the room – he gave me a pound on many occasions and once a five-pound note. Strangely neither of us ever referred to what was going on. I just talked about the accounts and he busied himself with my leg and then gave me half a crown, ten shillings or more when he'd finished. I didn't think I was selling myself at all, but I began to think he might be about to go too far when I knocked on his door one day after receiving the usual summons.

I walked in and waited to be told where to sit, which was the usual routine.

'Do sit,' he said, pointing at a hard chair pulled up to the big round table.

I took my place and put the account books down in front of me. I noticed that his shirt was pulled out of his trousers and he looked oddly flustered and very red in the face. I can't remember exactly what he said but it was something like this:

'Do you have a boyfriend, Kat?'

Now it happened that I had started to see a boy at this stage so I said yes. I'd been told that boyfriends were allowed so long as they never called at the house so I wasn't worried that my confession would get me into trouble.

'What do you do with him?' asked Mr Barker.

'Well, we go walking, sir,' I replied. 'Sometimes we go to the cinema.'

'What else do you do together?' he said. 'Does he touch you?'

Now any modern girl would have told him to bugger off at this stage but I just couldn't do it.

'We have a kiss now and then,' I said.

'But does he touch you? Does he touch your legs? He must, I think, as you have such lovely legs.'

Now I really was stumped. I said nothing and could feel myself getting very red in the face.

Then he said, 'I think if I were your boyfriend I'd do much more than touch your leg, Kat.'

And with that he just stared at me. I couldn't go on with the accounts but I also couldn't think of a thing to say so I stared stupidly at the floor.

Then he said, 'Good. That's all in order. Would you send Mrs Charlton to see me?'

And off I went.

From then on he always asked odd questions. About my boyfriend, about my clothes, about what I wore at night. On one occasion he asked if I had freckles on my body. He asked how many and where they were. I made up some nonsense and said twelve or something equally ridiculous. He was delighted and began to make more excuses so that I would have to spend twenty minutes or half an hour with him once or even twice a week. Whatever he asked me I just made up something but the questions were all vaguely sexual.

During my last interview with him he said:

'Kat, tell me. How often do you go to the lavatory?'

I wanted desperately to laugh at this but I kept a straight face and said, 'Oh, at least five times a day.' I'd realised that making up silly answers took all the sting and embarrassment out of our encounters.

'Do you really?' he replied. 'Do you enjoy it?'

'I do,' I said. 'Very much.'

'So do I,' he replied and he smiled at me.

Soon after that he asked me to leave the room and on my way out he gave me a ten-shilling note. That was our last interview.

He stopped asking me to see him because, as Mrs Charlton explained, a doctor had been called in a few days later after Mr Barker started going to the lavatory behind the sofa in his sitting room, and he wasn't just urinating on the carpet.

After that nurses came to the house. They changed now and then and sometimes there was one, sometimes two. It was rumoured that Mr Barker had had a stroke or a series of small strokes or he had some sort of rapidly deteriorating illness. When I occasionally saw him in the garden he was always in his old coat and seemed perfectly happy sweeping up the leaves – but always with a nurse nearby. In the final months before he died a middle-aged couple arrived at the house and everything changed. Their name was also Barker but I never found anything else out about them. I expect they were relatives of the old man but no one ever said and no one in the village knew them. They began to live in the house but Mrs Barker never came to see me or the housekeeper. She sent all her instructions down via the butler. I didn't mind the change. I carried on cooking and for the next few years we led a quiet life until just before the war began when the housekeeper retired and suggested to Mr and Mrs Barker that I should take over from her.

It had taken fifteen years and more but at last I'd got where I'd always wanted to be. I was formally offered the job this time and told I would get much better wages. To people of a different generation a housekeeper is still a servant but for me it was the difference between being a nobody and being a somebody.

Chapter 35

But if I'd only just become a somebody below stairs I never felt anything but a somebody in my free time and for a year or two before the war started I'd been having some fun away from work.

It was while old Mr Barker was still alive that I met my first serious boyfriend. I'd had an occasional fling with boys I met at the village dances when I'd been at the old house. I remember several times going to dances with Netta or Nessa or with both of them. I was very proud of my dancing although I'd never had a lesson. Netta, Nessa and I danced with each other late in the evenings in the house if there was no dance to go to and we'd take turns to be the man.

But I wanted a real boyfriend. I don't mind admitting that I used to like kissing boys if I got the chance and at those dances I remember the boys could hardly keep their eyes off us. They were like flies who'd just seen jam for the first time. People think we were all terrified about sex then and prudish. Well maybe some of us were but there were intelligent girls too who knew all about sex despite being servants because then, as now, sex was everywhere. We'd got past the silly Victorian attitude that meant you had to pretend babies were made by kissing or by a stork coming down a chimney. And though many houses banned boyfriends even that was beginning to change. As I've said, in Mr Barker's employ boyfriends were tolerated so long as they didn't come to the house.

For all our fears about pregnancy and getting the sack, there was an even bigger fear: the terror that we'd never get a boyfriend. Those who wanted to escape the drudgery of below stairs often married the first person who asked them and then they ended up exchanging drudgery at work for drudgery at home.

Other servant girls definitely got married in the desperate hope that they would at last be treated as grown-ups.

I didn't worry a bit about getting married because I had a different ambition, but I wouldn't have minded if the right man came along. What I wanted more than anything was to have some fun when I wasn't at work and that need to have fun was all centred on boys.

The truth is we were the same as girls throughout the ages. We had to pretend to be cool and uninterested, especially in the physical side of things, but underneath it all we were raring to go and just as keen as the boys. We loved the idea of being kissed – at least, all the maids I ever worked with did – and we loved the idea of doing more. I remember one boy I met at a dance with Nessa. I talked to a terrible boy who thought I should be interested in a thirty-minute talk on how tractor engines worked, and I got so fed up listening to him that I decided to give him a kiss without waiting to see if he wanted one. He was very pretty and I thought a kiss would shut him up! I'm sure he thought I was a disgracefully forward girl but he seemed delighted at the time and I thought, who cares? Even then I thought there was far too much prudishness. I liked to call a spade a spade. After that dance I went for a walk across the fields with engine boy and we lay down. I remember what a warm still night it was.

I remember too how my lips felt bruised for days afterwards but at the time I got very excited and only just managed to stop him doing everything. I'm not ashamed at all to admit I loved it but I knew that I was bound to be unlucky and that I would get pregnant so I stopped him just in time.

Chapter 36

I lost touch with Nessa and Netta after a few years with Mr Barker but I made friends with the village postman's daughter, Lily, who used to help him with the deliveries. She and I used to go into town on my night off. Lily was my great friend in those years with Mr Barker.

Barker was in many ways a very good employer as I've already explained. He may have mildly interfered with us girls, but on the good side he insisted the staff should each have two afternoons off a week, which was very rare in those days, one afternoon being the norm. Also your half days really were half days. There were no sneaky tricks to keep you on late as there were in many houses. I was always allowed to down tools immediately after lunch and leave the kitchen to Poppet. In many houses you couldn't leave for your half day until a certain amount of work had been done, which was a crafty way to make sure you didn't get as much time off as you should – but not at Mr Barker's. At his house you always got your full time and I'll always be grateful to him for that.

So I would meet Lily the postman's daughter and we would get the bus into Leicester and go to the dances. And it was at a dance that I met Micky the boxer.

At first I thought Micky was just spinning a bit of a yarn about being a champion boxer. I was used to boys spinning a yarn and making up all sorts of tales about how great they were at one thing or another so at first I didn't really think he was a boxer at all. I should have known different from the muscles – and the state of his nose!

There were several dance halls in Leicester back then. Some were tiny and shabby, others bigger and almost grand, but all over the town they drew girls like a magnet and they drew them in from the countryside round about which is how we got there. Country girls didn't want to go for walks or bicycling. They wanted the town and the lights. Even for a city girl like me the lure of the countryside had faded a bit after I'd had a decade and more of it and I began to long again for the city. For now the dances in Leicester were enough.

So there I was with Lily the postman's daughter. We were standing at the side of one of the bigger dance halls, both in our new dresses. We'd danced with several men and we were gossiping about them.

'God, look at that one over there. Isn't he gorgeous?' said Lily. She pointed to a very slim boy who was a bit on the short side, but had lovely dark curly hair and what we used to call film-star good looks. He had a sort of brooding expression with deep-set eyes and a strong chin. We watched him on and off for ages and not once did he smile. I think boys saw too much smiling as a sign of weakness. They liked to look mean and moody and this fella was busting a gut to keep it up!

Very few girls ever went up to a boy and asked for a dance. I think it might have happened more if we'd been able to drink but most of the dance halls had no alcohol. We used to try staring at boys we fancied so that's what Lily started to do with the dark-haired boy on the other side of the room.

'It's not bloody working,' she said after a while, looking genuinely put out.

'He's probably short-sighted,' I said.

'Don't be a cow!' she said, but laughing. 'How could anyone that good-looking have bad eyes?'

Then I noticed that the young man Lily fancied was talking to a few other young lads and at least some of them were looking our way. I thought maybe one of the others would ask Lily to dance.

We watched them for a bit longer then gave up and looked around and thought of other things. Then I felt a tug on my arm and when I looked round there was a big brute of a fellow standing next to me. He had cropped hair and a flattened nose. I looked round for Lily and there she was staring almost open-mouthed at the man talking to me. I tried to make a face at her as if to ask her to say something to get me out of a jam, but she was speechless.

The tough-looking boy said: 'I hope you don't mind me asking but do you fancy a dance?'

The difference between his appearance and his way of speaking was almost shocking as he looked a terrible roughneck. In fact he was as polite as the king of England if not quite as well spoken.

I couldn't think of a reason to say no so I smiled – I looked sick Lily told me later – and stepped on to the floor with him.

Well, for a big man he was quite the little twinkle-toes. He swept me around that floor like a professional.

When the dance finished he dropped me back with Lily who, so far as I could see, was still staring stupidly at me.

'Can I get you a drink?' he said and I thought, he wants to get me drunk, until I remembered they didn't sell alcohol.

'Just an orange or something I meant,' he said.

I told him I'd have a lemonade and off he went.

Now this was by no means the first time I'd been chatted up by a boy. I'd even had sex with one or two boys just to see what it was like. And I will tell you what it was like – it was a fuss about nothing. At least it was the first few times I tried it. A load of grunting and panic for about a minute, but that may have been because it was in the corner of a field or round the back of a barn!

So Micky – he'd told me his name by now – and I stood at the edge of the dance floor sipping our drinks. Lily just stared at me, making it clear she wasn't planning to say anything while Micky was there. I couldn't think of anything to say to either of them but I wasn't feeling shy exactly. It was more that I wasn't sure I wanted to encourage this King Kong of a man who was standing next to me and not wandering off as boys usually did after a dance. I'd hoped for a classically handsome date, not a bruiser! Maybe he'll just go away, I thought.

Then Micky said, 'My friend likes your friend.'

'Does he?' I said. 'You mean Lily?'

'Lily. He really fancies her. Shall I get him to come over?'

'If you like,' I said.

'What have you done?' said Lily in a panic as he went off to get his friend.

'I thought you liked him,' I said.

'I do but it's embarrassing.'

Girls always liked to make a big drama out of these things and Lily was no exception.

'Don't worry,' I said. 'There will be four of us and we'll get away in half an hour.'

And that's what we did.

They came over and we made embarrassing small talk for about twenty minutes and then, because Lily looked as if she was rooted to the spot just because a man was chatting her up, I said we'd have to go. It didn't look too bad because it was getting late anyway.

'Will we see you next week?' said Micky.

'I don't know,' I said, thinking I mustn't seem too keen. 'You might. All depends on how we feel about you when we've had time to think.'

Micky laughed at that and said: 'Try to come the same evening next week and we'll go out for a bit.'

All the next week I wondered what he meant by 'a bit'!

Chapter 37

I quickly realised that being a housekeeper is all about looking and sounding serious. Employers tended to expect you not to smile too much – that looked too frivolous – and when you were dealing with staff or money the trick was to frown a fair bit. And they really liked you to walk about as if you were suspicious of all the staff and every stranger who came within half a mile of the front door. In short you were supposed to be an old harridan, which was difficult for someone like me who was still in her thirties. The butler and the housekeeper were like bookends, really; they both had to keep up the pretence – and it was a pretence – that they found their work required absolute seriousness.

The butler at Mr Barker's house was called Tom Savile and I got to know him well once I became housekeeper and I can tell you he really was serious.

When I first took over and we had our initial meeting he looked down his nose at me. He thought I was too young for the job. One of the qualifications for housekeeper seemed to be that you were middle-aged or, even better, positively ancient.

My new wonderfully exciting job involved keeping good order among the female servants and making sure all the tradesmen's bills added up and the other servants' wages were paid in the right amount and on time.

Dealing with the tradesmen was a revelation for me. I was used to people treating me more or less as a nobody, but once I became housekeeper tradesmen in particular behaved towards me as if I was royalty! I loved it. They would virtually grovel to me.

I remember Mr Evans the butcher came to the house within days of my being appointed. I had no idea how news had reached him but when the maid knocked on my door one morning and told me he wanted to see me I remembered how he had once walked past me in the kitchen as if I was the house cat. Now it was very different.

I told the maid to show him in. He came into my room grinning so much he could hardly speak. He took his cap off and held it almost desperately in his hands while doing a series of little bows.

'Good morning, Mrs Clifford,' he said. 'Just wanted to make sure everyone is happy with everything.' He then did a few more bobs with his head and began shifting from foot to foot as if he needed the lavatory.

I couldn't resist teasing him a little.

'Thank you for coming to see me,' I said in my loftiest tones. 'I seem to remember one or two incidents in the past where there were difficulties.'

I stopped there and he looked terrified. There hadn't been any difficulties at all but I remembered how he'd walked past me as if I didn't exist when I was a lowly kitchen maid.

'Er . . . I'm sure we can . . . Perhaps a bottle of Madeira?'

Offering a little inducement like this was common among the tradesmen but I thought on this occasion I should say no so I pretended I didn't know what he meant and said, 'Well, I'm sure we can iron out any little difficulties in future. Thank you for coming to see me.'

And with that he left. No sooner had I got my revenge in this way than I felt rather bad about it and resolved to be nice to the other people with whom I would have to deal from now on.

The most important part of my new job, apart from dealing with the tradesmen, was to account for every penny and be able at any time to show my employer what had been spent that month, that year or over the past two or three years. So it was what they called a position of trust and coming via the kitchen corner, as we used to say, I was very lucky to have made it to housekeeper at all. I was probably a pain in the neck for poor old Savile the butler because I was much younger than he was and I could hardly conceal my delight at getting the job.

In fact it was obvious at the beginning that he thought it an outrage that someone like me should have a job so close in status to his, but there was nothing he could do about it.

At our first meeting Savile launched into a terrible, pompous speech.

'I know you haven't done this before and I will do my best to help you,' he said. 'You will need help of course but I am prepared to give it if you are prepared to take it.'

And on he went like that for the next ten minutes.

When he'd finished I tried to stay calm and not laugh.

'I'm always grateful for help, Mr Savile, and will certainly come to you if I need it,' I replied, 'but I don't expect I will be too much of a nuisance for you as your job and mine are so different. I will keep at the books and I know you will take care of the pantry.'

I hadn't intended that as a put-down but Savile looked really angry and I suppose it did sound like I was telling him to mind his own business. It was as if I'd said, 'Well, I can add up and all you can do is polish the silver!'

He went a bit red, made a noise in his throat that sounded like 'harrumph' and then we parted. I will say one thing for him. I'd more or less told him where to get off, but I don't think he ever held it against me, especially as he saw that the Barkers came gradually to rely on me. I think in some ways he admired the fact that I stuck up for myself.

Chapter 38

In addition to the house where Savile and I worked the Barkers had another, much bigger house in Northamptonshire so we were often left to our own devices as they moved between the two establishments – 'establishment' was one of those words that servants used in those days to make their jobs sound more important than they really were.

We might have a few days or a weekend when there was very little to do and then the family would turn up with twenty people to buy and cook for.

The Barkers had some interesting parties and as housekeeper I saw a lot more of what went on at them than I ever had when I'd been in the kitchen. I always thought of myself as flitting about the house like a ghost – not as visible as members of the family but not invisible like so many of the servants. I was even allowed to look at members of the family if I passed them on the stairs or in the hall so long as I did it with a deferential nod.

The first few parties I experienced as housekeeper were dinner parties and weekend affairs where the men played billiards and stood around smoking and talking about cars and racing. Meanwhile the women walked in the garden and gossiped. The family kept up the old tradition of men and women separating for an hour or so after dinner.

But then came a party that I wasn't likely to forget in a hurry.

It was about a year or two after the war started, when most people had given up any idea of having fun and there was a feeling that we were all doomed because the Germans were bound to invade and murder us all. This feeling of general gloom meant that when there was a bit of fun people tended to go completely wild.

It was a weekend party. The family had been away for a few days but we knew eight or ten were coming from Friday to Monday and we made sure we contacted the tradesmen in plenty of time to get as much food as we could, given that rationing was on. We could always get things that were unavailable to most people because the family knew local farmers. Meat was never in short supply and there was still a massive stock of wine from before the war.

When the guests arrived the butler answered the door while I hovered in the background. Servants were never introduced to visitors so Savile quietly took the men's coats while I supervised the women's as they were given to one of the housemaids. In a really grand house this would have all been done by the footmen, but footmen were a threatened species by this time except among the nobility.

The family and guests disappeared into the drawing room and the butler summoned the hall boy to help with the various bags. Soon everything had been sorted in the guests' bedrooms and we went back downstairs to make sure dinner was in preparation.

I had little to do at this time but Cook was in a frenzy of activity. I usually retreated at such times to my room – which was actually a set of rooms with a bedroom and a small sitting room and fire. It was known as the housekeeper's closet, I don't know why but there it is.

It was at moments like this for the rest of my career that I knew I'd made the right move. Why anyone would want to remain a cook indefinitely absolutely defeated me. Cook always had the worst of it when there were guests because she was always judged by her last meal. If she made a blunder everyone complained and no one remembered that the previous two hundred meals she had made were perfect.

And it was at the dinner that the weekend party started to go badly wrong.

I knew the kitchen was working flat out but I was in my room sitting by the fire and reading the paper, having made sure all the account books were up to date with wages and bills – I checked them nervously almost every evening. Then there was a knock on my door and it was the maid, Poppet.

'Cook's gone off,' she said.

'What?' I answered, not believing what she had just said.

'She's furious and she's gone to her mother's.'

I quickly followed her out and along the corridor to the kitchen. Immediately I realised that the main course had still to be served and, just as Poppet had said, Cook had vanished.

The cook was relatively new and had taken over from me when I became housekeeper. She had seemed unusually even-tempered to me during previous crises – there were regular crises in the kitchen – but this time whatever had happened had been too much for her. I found out from Poppet that Cook had been upset by a message conveyed from upstairs that the first course had not been what they had asked for.

I had no idea how that had happened, but we could deal with it later. For now we just had to get the main course on the table. I grabbed an apron and got Poppet to help me and soon the food was being rushed up to the dining table as if nothing had happened. Luckily for us it had been almost ready when Cook had bolted. We made a reasonable job of serving it, but the butler was furious and said he would have Cook sacked.

'We must wait and see why she ran off,' I said. 'It can't just be because upstairs has complained. They have complained before and nothing like this happened.'

This was one of the few times in service when I felt very angry. I wasn't angry with Cook, at least not then, but with Savile who instead of making the best of it got in the way and made things worse. While Poppet and I served up the food he stood in the middle of the kitchen moaning and threatening, and what good was that?

'Typical bloody man,' mumbled Poppet and I laughed despite everything because this was the first time I ever heard Poppet say anything spirited. But even after the crisis was averted Savile kept coming back into the kitchen blustering and complaining.

'She deserves the bloody push for this,' he said. 'She should be put out the bloody door, bag and baggage together.' He was absolutely fuming.

'You leave her alone,' I said. 'I look after the female staff, not you. We don't know what might have happened. I will talk to her when she comes back.'

He gave me a furious look but said no more because he knew he did not have the power to sack anyone.

I'd never rushed about so much as I did that evening and I'm not sure the family even realised that something had gone wrong. Savile was all for telling them, but I said we should wait.

Sure enough I heard Cook come in at about eleven when the family were having a final few drinks in the drawing room. I went out to meet her.

'I'm so sorry, Mrs Clifford,' she said. 'I had bad news from home as well as complaints from upstairs. Had a bit of a fit. It won't happen again.'

She looked extremely upset so, without saying a word, I waved her out of the kitchen and into my rooms. She looked almost in shock so I poured her a glass of port and, after taking a big sip, she explained that her brother had been injured in a car accident in Leicester and the boy who had come to tell her had said he was at death's door. In fact he was in hospital but not nearly as bad as that. So Cook was back and the crisis was over.

Or at least it was till the next day.

The truth about domestic service is that for long periods nothing much of any interest happens. You got more of a sense of this as housekeeper because in many ways you had fewer day-to-day tasks than any of the other servants.

That and status were the great attractions of the job but also in many way the great disadvantage. You could never just wander off, but so long as you kept the staff from fighting or leaving or setting fire to the house and so long as the books added up, you could put your feet up in your own little room, read the paper, poke the fire now and then and relax. But in the long run this could be very boring. Then just when it seemed the routine would never change, something surprising would happen or there would be a crisis.

After the incident with Cook I should have realised that this was likely to be a weekend to remember. After months of not much happening at all everything was about to get completely out of hand.

The nightmare started with a vengeance on the Saturday night, the day after Cook had run off. We knew that Mr and Mrs Barker and their guests were having a fancy-dress party and this involved inviting a few of their local friends to make up a party of about twenty people in all.

This seemed pretty straight forward. I went to see Cook and checked that she was happy now and able to cater for all the other guests. I had already discussed with her earlier in the week all the extra food we would need for the weekend and how much it would all cost. Everything had been delivered and Poppet and Cook knew what to do. It should have been easy.

Things started well enough. The family and their guests gathered in the big drawing room early that Saturday evening. It was a fancy-dress party and word filtered down that one woman was dressed as an admiral of the fleet, while another, male guest was dressed as Little Bo Peep and yet another had kitted himself out as Isadora Duncan the famous dancer. It seemed the women had dressed as men and the men as women. One woman I recall seeing wore doublet and hose and a long cape, another was dressed as a Roman emperor. Another guest had blackened her face to look like a minstrel.

As the evening wore on more guests arrived and the butler seemed to be always at the door letting them in. Each time he came back down I heard him complaining loudly at what was happening. At one point he came to my room and said, 'You should see the bloody people arriving. Poofs and queers the way they're dressed.'

'It's just a fancy-dress party,' I said.

'Yes but why do the men have to dress as women? It's not natural.'

'Well, they can be as unnatural as they like,' I replied. 'Because they pay our wages.'

'Well, I don't like it,' said Savile.

I crept up the stairs now and then and along the corridor just to listen to the screeches coming from the drawing room. That might sound an odd thing to do but the housekeeper was supposed to be all eyes and ears and I was worried that something – or someone – might get damaged.

The noise grew steadily louder as time passed. Savile, red-faced, angry and sweating, was forced to carry large amounts of wine up from the cellar. He treated the wine in the cellar as if it was his own property and was upset when the better bottles were drunk by the family. But this was much worse.

'They'll drink the bloody lot the way they are going,' he said.

I don't think he minded a bit that Mr and Mrs Barker might be upset by the consumption of so much of their wine. He just hated the idea that the precious bottles he turned regularly and entered in his book were disappearing as if they were just water or ginger beer.

Servants like Savile were typical of the sort who stayed throughout their careers with the same family. They ended up thinking that the things they looked after were their own property and they resented it when the family changed their usual habits.

So after Friday's business with Cook I now had to contend with an angry Savile. Like all good servants he kept his anger for downstairs and presented a cool, unperturbed face to the family and their guests.

I first knew something was very wrong when I heard a tremendous crash followed by the sound of Savile running along the hall.

'Someone's knocked over a table,' he shouted. 'And there's drink all over the floor and smashed glass.'

Here we go again, I thought. I grabbed Poppet and ran upstairs with Savile close behind.

The drawing room was like a scene from a madhouse. There were couples on the sofas and on the floor; there were couples slumped in corners and across tables. As the men were dressed as women and the women as men it was hard to tell who was who. I saw one couple rolling around on the floor kissing passionately. But as I watched I realised it was not a man and a woman but two girls.

I tried to find Mr and Mrs Barker but Savile told me they had gone to bed and left the others to get on with it.

This was a pretty pickle, and unheard of in my experience.

We tried to clear up the mess but the guests were so rowdy it was really difficult even moving among them.

'Who's this?' said one young man seeing me pass. He lurched towards me and reached out and grabbed one of my breasts. I wasn't particularly offended because he was drunk and that's the sort of thing men do when they are drunk. I pushed him off and carried on across the room. Another man made a grab at me and tried to get me to dance with him, but he was so drunk it was easy for me to push him off.

But what a dilemma.

We could hardly wake Mr and Mrs Barker and we could hardly order the dozen or so guests still there at two in the morning to leave.

Savile and I decided that rather than go back downstairs we would stand discreetly at the edge of the drawing room where most of the guests were still dancing, shouting, singing or just lying on the floor or on top of each other. We thought they might feel uncomfortable with us watching them with what we hoped were stern (but not disrespectful) looks on our faces, but it didn't work.

I wasn't the least embarrassed, however. I didn't feel awkward or even remotely angry. I just thought what fools these people were making of themselves when the rest of the time they liked to think they were so superior. I'd never really liked alcohol because I saw what it did to people – Paddington in my childhood had been awash with drunks – and I suppose that in this sense at least I was a bit prissy!

So we stood and watched. I went back to my room a few times and to the kitchen to make sure the other servants weren't too worried by the noise and the disruption to our usual routine. Each time I returned to stand by Savile the drink still seemed to be flowing.

Savile was asked to bring up more wine every few minutes and what could he do but bring it. He was furious and deliberately took as long as he could. He would also bring the cheapest wine and stand with it at the door to the drawing room hoping that neither it, nor he, would be noticed.

At one point a drunken guest lurched up to Savile.

'Where's that bottle I asked you to bring up?' he demanded.

'I'm so sorry, sir,' Savile replied. 'I think I misheard and I have returned to make sure it was the white Burgundy you required.'

Savile knew exactly what the young man had asked for but this was one of his delaying tactics. He did it repeatedly and the guests were so drunk they only occasionally became angry at all the delays.

When I returned to my station by Savile's side at about three in the morning most of the lights had been turned off. I waded through bottles and overturned furniture and sleeping bodies to the far end of the room, which was a large dog-leg and therefore could not be seen from our position at the main door. As I walked through I saw two of the guests having sex on the sofa. The sofa was exactly at the point where the sitting room turned left so I was right next to them before I saw anything. There they were, Little Bo Peep and the Roman emperor, and despite my exhaustion and bad temper I found it impossible not to laugh. They looked so ridiculous it was difficult to be offended. They were going at it with such enthusiasm that they didn't notice me at all and when I think back all I remember is thinking that Little Bo Peep appeared to have a remarkably hairy bottom.

Next to the couple having sex stood a man dressed in a shabby and very droopy pair of undershorts. He smiled and waved at me and then turned his gaze back to the couple on the sofa.

I didn't mention any of this to Savile when I got back to the door where he continued to stand guard. I thought that might be the final straw. I knew what he'd say: 'And how am I supposed to get the stains out of the sofa?'

In one corner I noticed a huge pool of vomit and on the floor by the big fireplace was another couple fast asleep. Two figures dressed as Robin Hood and Maid Marion were arguing on another sofa and as I gazed around I really began to think it would never end.

I noticed Savile had disappeared again so I followed him downstairs. On the way along the servants' corridor I was forced to turn back by the sound of someone screaming for help.

I rushed to the drawing room and saw that an oil lamp on a table by the fireplace had been knocked over. The couple who had been asleep on the floor by the fireplace were frantically brushing burning oil off their costumes. A half-dressed girl stood a few feet away biting her nails and in floods of tears but rooted to the spot.

I helped put out the fire which was burning in small pools here and there on the floor. I ran as fast as I could and came back with two big copper cans of water. I took a particular pleasure in throwing one of the cans of water over the two guests – and then I threw the other can at them just to make sure.

By now I'd had enough and even at the risk of complaints reaching the ears of Mr and Mrs Barker, I decided it was time for the party to end.

I opened all the curtains and asked Savile to go down and wake the maid and ask her to help clear up. I also turned the lights on and that seemed to transform the scene. Even the drunkest among the guests began to come back to the real world, to blink, sit up and at least partially realise where they were and what they were doing.

Savile tore out through the door. I'd never seen him move so quickly but as he rushed across the hall I saw something extraordinary: he seemed to rise in the air and turn a slow-motion somersault before landing with a thump on his back. He had slipped on the patch of water I'd slopped out of one of my cans.

I heard an agonised shout from a man who was always reticent, as are all butlers: 'Oh, me bollocks!' Amid the chaos I wept with laughter.

Two minutes later the maid flew into the room and we pretended the family had asked us to clear up and chivvied the guests off to bed or out of the house.

The two who had been lying by the fire had disappeared to the bathroom, one or two of the others were trying to find their clothes or were pretending to look as if nothing untoward had happened.

All the high jinks had come to an end as if someone had thrown a switch and within half an hour the guests had either left the house in their motor cars or crept upstairs and we were left with the most awful scene I think I have ever witnessed.

Despite the mess they had made or perhaps because of it not one guest even glanced at Savile and me as they left. Of course they were all very drunk but I thought how much like naughty schoolchildren they were. And how odd that Mr and Mrs Barker should have gone to bed and left them to it!

I think the madness may have had something to do with the fact that the war was on and this sort of party was almost unheard of during those years. People were desperate to have a bit of fun when fun was in short supply and things were perhaps bound to get out of hand.

And there was one last surprise in store for us. When all the guests had left or gone to bed I opened a storeroom just inside the green baize door that separated the servants' part of the house from the rest of it and inside I found a girl lying unconscious and wearing only a soldier's tunic – the rest of her was completely naked. When I gently woke her she had no idea how she had got into the storeroom, which was really just a walk-in cupboard, nor what had happened to her; but I'm as certain as I can be that some of the men had raped her while she was unconscious.

After she got to her feet she said, 'Oh, I'm so sore,' and she pressed her stomach low down.

I saw blood on her legs and I knew what that meant. I said, 'Did anything happen to you?' It was a stupid question but it just came out before I could think.

'No, nothing, really,' she mumbled. 'Please don't say anything.'

She can't have been more than nineteen or twenty.

'Would you get me a towel and some aspirins?' she said in a weak, tearful voice. I got both and then took her to her room where she got into bed and began crying.

'Would you like me to get Mrs Barker?' I asked.

'No please don't,' she said. 'It's all my fault.'

I so wanted to comfort her but the barriers of class and status made it almost impossible.

In typical silly English style all I could think then was to offer to get her a cup of tea. I sent the maid up with it ten minutes later but she reported that the young lady was now fast sleep.

If she had been raped nothing more was ever said about it and that was so typical of the time. Rape was still seen very much as the girl's fault, especially if she had been drinking, and it was almost as bad then to admit to having been raped as it was to be accused of rape.

The poor maid was left with a terrible job the next day. I had to make an inventory of all the damage – broken vases and pictures, cigarette burns all over the rugs and even on the curtains and walls, a broken table and perhaps strangest of all several missing ornaments, including valuable silver boxes and other trinkets. It seemed that the family's friends were quite happy to steal from them.

Several people had been sick on the floor and one of the big main windows was cracked.

Over the days that followed neither Mr nor Mrs Barker ever mentioned the party to a member of staff. When I had my next meeting with Mrs Barker she asked if there were any problems below stairs and she also asked me to make an inventory of the entire contents of the house. I assumed this was because she was worried about what had gone missing at the party, but I was wrong. She had very different reasons and these were to change my life.

Chapter 39

Micky the boxer and I were getting on wonderfully well. I'd always enjoyed going out with Lily and having the odd fling with boys we'd met, but Micky was my first steady, as we used to say. Other boyfriends I'd met at dances and kissed and flirted with; sometimes, as I've said, I even went a bit further with them. I was happy with all that but I was in my thirties now and rather liked the idea of having a real boyfriend even though I didn't think it would lead anywhere ultimately.

By that I mean I never thought I would marry. I was too wary and too independent and, unlike most women, I enjoyed being on my own and I certainly didn't want the sort of man who expected to be waited on hand and foot once he was married. So that pretty much ruled out every male in the country!

Men and marriage were fun and great if you wanted children but since all men are children really and never grow up there was no point expecting much from them in the way of money or loyalty. Working-class men, even tough boxers, expected their women to look after them, not the other way round.

It was the middle and upper classes who liked the idea of a delicate creature on a sofa showered with expensive gifts and looked after like an invalid from morning till night.

Working-class women in my day had to rely on themselves as I had always done. But even with all that in mind Micky and I had some great days out and he wasn't a bad old bugger really.

Lily and I had met him and Danny Boy – Danny was his good-looking friend – in the same dance hall again a week later and it seemed perfectly natural to me to go over and smile and say hello, though Lily was not so sure.

'You did turn up then,' said Micky, which was a statement of the bloody obvious, though I resisted the temptation to say that. He looked very pleased all the same. We talked a bit more and then he asked me what I did and where I lived.

'I'm a housekeeper,' I said.

'Get out of it,' he said, laughing. 'You can't be. You're making it up.

'Danny, listen to this, she says she's a housekeeper. Did you ever hear the like?'

Suddenly I felt real rage that they were laughing at what I did so I said, 'If you think it's so funny then you can entertain yourselves tonight.' I turned and began to walk away from them.

Quick as you'd expect a boxer to be, Micky was by my side.

'I didn't mean to offend you,' he said and he looked like he really meant it. 'I got carried away. The truth is you are far too pretty and far too young to be a house-keeper. It was my ignorance made me laugh.'

'That's all right,' I said. I was mollified straight away because Micky had a great gift for sounding like he meant what he said – and even sometimes really meaning it. And if he thought I seemed an unlikely housekeeper I thought he seemed a most unlikely boxer so I wanted to find out about him. The oddest thing was that he seemed far too well spoken to be what he claimed to be.

'You're in no position to talk about people's jobs anyway,' I said as we walked back over to the others. 'You speak like the people I work for, yet you say you're a boxer.'

'I'm an amateur boxer,' he said. 'The slightly posh sort. I do it for the fun of it – and for the money. I was very good at it at school so I thought why not make some money at it. The rest of the time, Danny and me, we do odd jobs.'

God, I thought, just like my bloody mum I end up with an odd-job man. The phrase 'odd jobs' was always code for being a bit of a layabout with a liking for the dogs and horses thrown in. But never mind. I had no intention of marrying Micky. I just wanted a laugh and to have some fun before I was an old woman.

It was during the two years I was with Micky that I realised it was necessary to lead a double life if you wanted to be a good domestic and have fun away from work. You could be one thing outside work and another much more serious person when you were in your official role, just so long as the two parts of your life never overlapped.

Only once did I make a mistake and try to mix the two.

Chapter 40

I'd been seeing Micky for around six months and we were definitely in the honeymoon phase. I don't mean we'd actually been wed or anything, just that we were in that early period when everything about your loved one seems perfect and things you will eventually find really irritating seem charming and funny or just plain lovable.

So we were in love I suppose, but our relationship didn't mean much if you added up the amount of time we spent together. We never went on holiday or even away for the weekend. Holidays were for the well-off, a bit like knowing how to speak French.

We used to meet, go for a walk, lie in the fields in summer with lots of kissing and more – I'd been into Leicester for the equipment! – and in winter we'd have fish and chips together and go for more walks. But when I look back I realise that, in those early months, I would have happily sat staring at paint dry with Micky. The reasons I fell for him are hard to remember now. He was certainly very funny in a dry sort of way and he was quite an impressive-looking man from a physical point of view. From all that fighting I suppose. Lily put it well when she said:

'Fuck me, Kat, he's like a brick-built shithouse.'

Women far more often go for looks than people think. We're supposed to be interested in deeper qualities. Well, I can tell you that in my experience that's just not true or at least it wasn't back then. No one wanted to go out with a thin little bookish man who was no good with his hands. That was probably fine if he was a millionaire or a lord but if you have no money, no career and not much education all you have to show for yourself is your physical appearance.

That's why you sometimes saw the daughters of some big local landowner walking round in all sorts of eccentric rags. They didn't need to rely on their appearance because they had the status of being somebody, rags or no rags.

Servant girls, on the other hand, would get dressed up to the nines to go out for the day because they only had their looks to trade with.

The posh girls would say, 'How common!' when they saw servant girls dressed to look glamorous but they didn't understand that clothes and appearance are all you have if you are a nobody.

So I always got dressed up for Micky. As housekeeper, I had enough money to buy all the clothes I wanted and I had some lovely things. I even broke the golden rule – and bought myself silk knickers. In the old days when I'd started work, silk knickers were strictly forbidden for servants, but by the late 1940s no one would have dared tried to impose a rule like that. So with what I liked to think of as my film-star good looks and Micky the size of Tarzan we must have looked a proper pair when we were out walking.

Lily had quickly fallen out with Danny so our days as a foursome didn't last and it was towards the end of what I call the honeymoon period that I made a mistake that could have cost me my job.

I met Micky once when I had been given the whole weekend off. I didn't ask for extra time off that often but the atmosphere in the servant world was changing and employers were definitely becoming kinder and more generous. So when I asked the mistress she said yes almost without a murmur. Twenty years earlier she would have said, 'Why do you need this time? Where are you going? We can only allow this if you need to see your family.'

But no one said that kind of thing any more and besides I was the housekeeper not the skivvy in the kitchen. Micky and I planned to spend the whole of Saturday together. I would then go back to the house late as I liked as I had a key and there was no curfew, and then I would spend Sunday in my rooms with my feet up. Much as I loved Micky I never really wanted to spend more than one day with him at a time because we had nowhere to go!

So we spent the day doing what we usually did and then around nine o'clock in the evening, after we'd seen a film in the town, I told him I would have to be getting back. This didn't usually bother Micky at all, but this time it was different.

'Why don't I see you back to the house?' he said.

'Why would you want to do that?' I said. 'You'd have to get back to the town again. It's ten miles or more.'

He gave me what I later thought was a very sneaky look, but then smiled.

'I'd like to see where you spend so much time. I'll walk you to the gate and then I'll be off.'

No harm in that, I thought, and I'll have someone to talk to on the bus.

But a little bit of me was nervous even at the idea of him coming to the gate. It wasn't that I was ashamed of him; it was more that like most servants of the day I kept work and pleasure strictly separate. I didn't want some besotted boyfriend hanging around and mooning over the park gate. The boss would not have liked that at all and it would not sit well with the image of a housekeeper as a silent, serious, matronly figure gliding discreetly from room to room and then retreating to her closet and her knitting.

The bus dropped us at the end of the lane and we walked the last two hundred yards to the turn into the drive.

'Goodbye, Micky,' I said. 'I have to go now and I don't want the whole bloody house to see your boxer's nose peeping over the fence like a burglar.'

Micky laughed. 'Why don't you let me in to stay the night?'

'You must be joking,' I said. 'I knew you were up to something at the bus stop. You had that cheeky look on your face.'

I was angry because I'd suspected all along that having come so far, he wouldn't want to go home so late in the evening.

'You'll get me the bloody sack,' I hissed.

'Come on, just this once. Wouldn't you like to get one over on the old stiffs in there?'

'No I bloody wouldn't,' I said. 'I'm very comfortable where I am thank you and I can't take up boxing if I get the push.'

'You won't get the push you silly thing,' he said and put his arm around me. He gave me a kiss.

'Go on. Just this once. I want to see where you live when you are not with me.'

I was already wavering because I thought, we can't stand here all night arguing. Someone is bound to see us. Then, I think, a little devil momentarily took possession of me and I thought, Why not?

Part of me was fed up being so careful and so discreet and controlled the whole time. A big part of being a housekeeper was your demeanour – it was about seeming to be a very serious person and for that second in the lane I felt sick of being serious. In a moment of madness I said, 'I'll do it just this once, but I'm not making a habit of it.'

Once I'd agreed I was quite excited. It was like being a schoolgirl again and hopping the wag – I mean bunking off school and roaming the streets.

It was very dark as we walked carefully up the drive. Only once had I ever bumped into anyone else when I returned from a night out. Servants in the country tended to go to bed early as there was nothing else to do and they had to be up so early.

This was a very still night so we kept to the grass on the edge of the drive so our shoes could not be heard on the gravel. I could hear Mickey breathing heavily behind me and then, to my horror, as the house came into view, he started to giggle.

I turned around and stared at him. His face was contorted with the effort of suppressing his giggles.

'What's so bloody funny?' I whispered.

'Nothing,' came the slightly strangled reply. He was puce by now and could hardly get the words out.

I was furious and knew now that this was all a terrible mistake. I waited till Micky seemed to calm down a bit.

At last he said, 'The more I try not to laugh the more I want to.'

'If you don't stop right now and get a grip on yourself you'll be back out on the road,' I told him.

I was angry but somehow felt I couldn't go back on what we'd agreed.

*   *   *

We crept on and I think Micky was still struggling not to laugh. Then I heard a thump and the gasps of suppressed giggles stopped. I turned around and saw that Micky had tripped on the low metal rail that ran along a short stretch of the path. I'd forgotten to mention it to him. He lay at a funny angle, his head in a rhododendron bush and his legs splayed behind him. Now it was my turn to shove my fist in my mouth to stop myself laughing out loud.

I pulled him up and he hissed into my ear.

'My fucking shins are killing me. My leg is split in two!'

I gave him the sternest look I could muster in the circumstances and put my finger to my lips.

Why on earth I didn't abandon this mad scheme at this point I will never know, but I felt I'd gone too far and it wouldn't have been fair on Micky.

We made it to the servants' door at last and without further disasters and I dug about in my bag until I found my key. My hands were shaking. So much for the cool, calm housekeeper.

I stopped and listened carefully. Silence. I opened the door as quietly as I could. I knew the trick of sliding the key in carefully and then pulling the door knob towards me which reduced the sound of the click.

The corridor was in darkness, but I knew where the obstacles were and it was only a short distance along to my closet.

I reached back for Micky's hand and gripped it as tightly as I could so there was no chance he could slip off in the wrong direction. I was thoroughly shaken by now and convinced that someone would hear us, and that worst of all it would be Savile the butler.

I thought, If he sticks his head out the door now I will die with embarrassment. They won't have to sack me because I will be so ashamed I will never again show my face in the house. My breathing sounded horribly loud to me as we went the last few steps to the door of my rooms. It was like listening to a steam engine leaving St Pancras – or at least it was to me!

I got the door open, bundled Micky in and locked the bolt securely behind me.

'Don't move an inch,' I said.

'What's wrong?'

'Shhh!' I hissed. 'I want to hear if anyone is moving about.' I must have listened to the silence for the next minute or so. But there was nothing.

'Do you have anything to drink,' said Micky, who stretched and suddenly looked completely at ease.

'You must whisper,' I said. 'All the time.'

'All right, I can manage that,' he replied. 'But give me a drink to calm my nerves.'

I thought how funny that the great boxer should be terrified of being caught in his girlfriend's bedroom.

Once we'd turned the light on we sat side by side on the small leather sofa in my sitting room and tried to calm down.

'This is very nice,' he whispered.

'Thanks,' I said. 'None of it is mine.'

'Ah who cares. At least you get the use of it.' Micky

was always practical like this and never wanted to own anything at all so far as I could see. But the sad side of that was that he had no ambition to get beyond a boxer's life and no thought for the future. I knew he'd spend his life drifting from rented room to rented room, but that was just the way he was and there were many in those days who were just the same. The whole country, I once thought, is full of cheap boarding houses filled with middle-aged and retired men going nowhere.

Micky asked for a cup of tea and, polite to the last, asked if he could stretch out on the sofa.

'Help yourself to the sofa,' I said, 'but take your boots off. I'm not making tea at this time of night but you can have a glass of this.'

I opened a half-finished bottle of port and gave him a big slug of the stuff.

I let Micky stay this one time though I always regretted it afterwards. We went to bed together and it was lovely in some ways and bloody awful in others. It reminded me of sharing a bed with my brothers as a child. I hadn't hated it then but I never wanted to go back to it. Sleeping alone wasn't a question of being lonely; it was a luxury.

The sex part of my relationship with Micky was mostly fun, but not when every sound might be someone coming to knock on my door! By the time I heard the big clock upstairs strike two o'clock I thought', God, is he never going to stop! I was a bag of nerves again and constantly had to tell him to stop groaning and grunting and that just made him laugh. Afterwards when we tried to get some sleep it was impossible – anyone who has ever tried to sleep two in a small bed will know what I mean. At various times I woke with his elbow in my eye or he'd roll over quickly and butt me with his head. Then when I had finally dozed off comfortably he woke me with a shove and said I'd punched him in the head. I'd actually just rolled over with my arm out and it had landed on his head but with his boxing he thought he was under attack.

If we hadn't both been so tense all of this would have been funny. I laughed about it afterwards but not much at the time.

But there was worse to come. Just when I thought we'd got through the worst of it there was a loud knock on the main door of the house. I nearly jumped out of my skin. It was the most awful sound I have ever experienced. I was feeling guilty enough already but I knew I would now be found out. It would be an understatement to say that this was by far the worst moment of my life. If Micky was found in my rooms I would lose all that I had worked for. Why had I done it? It was so stupid. That little devil in me that I'd almost always managed to suppress had been given his head just enough to ruin me.

I heard doors opening and the butler's footsteps shuffling along the corridor. I couldn't move. I was normally so confident in everything I did but this was beyond me. I couldn't get Micky out without being seen because having been wakened like this the butler would be unlikely to go back to sleep and Micky had to be out before everyone else got up.

I heard the bolts go on the main door and my panic left me. I jagged Micky in the ribs but he hardly stirred. I hit him harder and hissed in his ear.

'You'll have to go.'

'What? What time is it? It's the middle if the night,' he said. 'You must be joking.'

'Someone may come to my room. Be quick or they'll find you here and I'll be finished.'

Micky finally came out of his daze and jumped out of bed. Even he began to look worried. As he hopped around looking for his shirt and socks I begged him to be quiet so I could hear what was happening outside. There was more shuffling and confused noises.

It was just starting to get light so I told Micky he would have to climb out the window and make a run for it. Maybe no one would knock on my door but I didn't want to risk it. I slowly opened the old sash window and of course it squawked and bawled fit to wake the dead. As Micky hesitated on the window sill I pushed him as hard as I could and just as you'd expect when you least need another disaster, the top sash slipped down as he was climbing through and hit him on the head.

'Jesus fucking Christ,' he said as he fell forward and the window pinned him down half in and half out of the room.

'It was the bloody window!' I whispered as I lifted

it off him. I got him out at last. I was sweating with terror by now. I told him to run and what a sight he made half dressed and his coat and trousers under his arm and tearing down the drive in the half light towards the road.

I gazed after him and tried to calm myself as he disappeared into the early morning gloom and I gradually brought the window down.

'Stop!' I heard a shout from the gardens. A whistle blew.

I'm sacked, I thought.

'Yes, you, stop!' came the shout again and then mingled shouts and other voices.

Oh God, I hope they don't catch him, I thought.

I looked around to make sure my rooms looked decent and that there was not a sign of Micky anywhere. And the first thing I saw were his shoes.

I'd seen a farce at the playhouse once with Micky and what had happened this night might easily have been turned into a play except that it wasn't funny at all for me at the time.

I hid his shoes and I tidied up a bit. I made sure the window was secure and just when I thought I was safe there came a knock on my door. It was the butler with a policeman behind him.

'It's the police,' said Savile.

'I can see that,' I said.

'Good morning, ma'am,' said the policeman trying to peer over Savile's shoulder.

'We had a report that someone was seen hovering

in the gardens tonight and I came to make sure everything was safe and sound. Have you heard anything?'

I prayed I was not blushing and said:

'No, I'm afraid I haven't heard a thing and I would have noticed anyone prowling around, I think, as I've had a bad night. I just couldn't get to sleep properly. I've been tossing and turning, but apart from the odd fox barking I haven't heard a peep.'

And that was that. They went away and I went back to bed and spent the next hour cursing my stupidity, convinced that Micky would be caught and confess everything and all my years of work would end in nothing. But by some miracle I got away with it and had a narrow escape. I never made the same mistake again. What was supposed to add a little excitement to life had robbed me of a night's sleep and made me age by about ten years.

Chapter 41

It's sad because that incident at the house made me cool a bit towards Micky. I don't think I ever thought of him as my partner for life, but I was somehow wary after that. This was very unreasonable of me I know as it wasn't Micky's fault. In truth I had made the mistake of trying to mix work and pleasure and the souring of our relationship was the price I paid.

We still saw each other on my days and occasional weekends off, but something had gone out of it. It was almost as if we had become friends, which is not a good thing when you want a passionate affair.

I think I was intrigued by Micky at the outset because I was surprised that a boxer could be quite so gentle. And I know he fancied me like mad because even after things began to go off he still couldn't keep his hands off me!

Once towards the end of our time together he became my great hero. It was several months after the near disaster of our night of passion in my closet. Micky was celebrating his birthday and he suggested we go to a restaurant in Leicester. Now there were very few restaurants in Leicester at that time although there were dozens of chip shops. I was extremely embarrassed that I'd managed to reach my thirties and had never been to a proper restaurant so I was looking forward to it.

We arrived and were shown to our table. I have no idea what sort of restaurant it was but it seemed like a very ordinary sort of chophouse to me. Micky thought it was the height of sophistication but as a result he lost all his normally jolly confidence and seemed quite subdued. Looking back I don't think it was the least bit posh but we were both so inexperienced we thought it was probably just like the Ritz. I felt a bit out of place and Micky sensed it and it made him even more uncomfortable. We had several knives and forks on the table in front of us and I had to whisper to Micky and explain why there were so many – and I only knew because I remembered from my kitchen days. He hadn't a clue and normally under these sorts of circumstances he would have made a joke but I could sense he felt he was about to be shown up – I mean made to look a fool in front of everyone – and I knew he would hate that.

The waiter sensed we were not comfortable and he made things worse by behaving in a slightly offhand way. But we did our best, ordered something to eat and then sat mostly hoping we wouldn't be noticed by the other diners. The truth was that this was not the sort of restaurant that servants and boxers ate in. I could tell immediately. It was for the middle classes. Not for the really well-to-do but for doctors and company directors, that sort of person. We stuck out like a sore thumb and in those days when you made a gaffe like this people might easily point it out to you. We decided not to have a pudding because Micky was in agonies in his only suit, which I knew he hated wearing, and I sensed that we should just go.

We ordered the bill, paid quickly and left.

'Christ I'm glad to get out of there,' said Micky. 'I've got bloody indigestion from being stared at and made to feel uncomfortable.'

'Don't worry,' I said. 'We won't give them our business any more. It's their loss!'

Micky laughed at that and we set off for the bus stop. We passed a public lavatory and Micky said he had to spend a penny so I stood and waited while he dashed in. Almost the instant he disappeared two young men approached me.

The first one said, 'How much, love?'

Now I'd grown up in a rough part of London but even with my background I hadn't a clue what he meant for a few seconds. Then the penny dropped.

'Bloody cheek,' I said. 'I'm not a working girl!'

I didn't take offence. After the stress of an hour in that bloody restaurant there was something almost comic about these two.

But for some reason they turned nasty. They'd probably been drinking, but one got one side of me and the other pinned me at the other side.

'Come on, we just want a kiss,' said the first.

'You'll get a smack if you don't hop it now,' I said. I would have given them a belt with my bag but I was still so surprised at what was happening that I thought they were just being cheeky. I was such an idiot that all I remember was thinking, I mustn't make a fuss or this will just get worse.

I didn't even shout for Micky. But he had been a long time and in a moment of panic I began to think he'd deserted me.

Then the bigger of the two men grabbed my arm and squeezed so hard it hurt. He and his friend began to pull me along the road. I knew that there was a field a short way along the road with a thick hedge. If they got me in there I would be in desperate trouble. Then I heard a voice.

'What do you two think you're doing?'

Micky was standing right in front of the three of us. I hadn't even seen him coming. The two men still thought they were in control of the situation because they smirked at each other, looked Micky up and down and were clearly thinking, You might be big but there are two of us.

I wanted to say to them, 'Look at Micky's nose you idiots – he's a bloody boxer!'

'Hop it, ugly, she's with us,' said the bigger of the two.

'What did you say?' said Micky and he suddenly looked very threatening. I had never seen that look on his face before.

The man then leaned forward until his face was right in front of Micky's face and, in a very slow, nasty voice he said, 'Piss off while you still can.'

Then everything paused for a instant before the figures in front of me began to move in what seemed to be slow motion. It was as if I was watching something on a stage.

Mickey completely changed. He did a strange little dance and lifted his fists till they were protecting his face and upper chest. For a second or two the little skipping dance continued and at the edge of my vision I could see the two men who still held my arms. Their mouths had almost fallen open in disbelief and they looked as if they were about to laugh. It was as if they were thinking, What's this bloke up to? Is he mad?

Then much faster than anyone could imagine, Micky's right arm shot out and there was an audible crack as his fist hit the bigger of my two attackers on the lower part of his face. He never made a sound. Not even a sigh. He just sank out of sight. I felt his grip vanish. Micky was still doing his little boxer's dance. The other fellow knew what was about to happen and he turned and ran like a hare down the road. Micky finished his little dance and put his fists down.

'Sorry I was a long time,' he said. 'That bloody restaurant food gave me a terrible stomach ache.'

I was too stunned to be angry with him but I said, 'I was nearly in trouble there.'

'No, you were fine,' said Micky. 'Just a couple of kids.'

We probably should have checked that the man Micky had knocked out was not too badly injured but Micky would have none of it.

'Serves him bloody right,' he said. As we walked along to the bus stop I looked back a few times and the man Micky had knocked down still hadn't moved from the ground. We climbed on to the bus and went back to Micky's digs.

Chapter 42

The war had been over for some time when the great shock in the Barker household came. I had prepared the inventory Mrs Barker had asked for with great care but it had taken weeks as the house was full of cupboards and closets and storerooms that were absolutely crammed with stuff. Most of it looked like rubbish to me but it could have been priceless for all I knew – and whatever I thought, it had to be listed in detail.

I remember not feeling any curiosity about why Mrs Barker wanted the inventory. I couldn't see anything sinister in it and even if I had suspected something was up I could hardly have refused to do it.

The list included some real oddities. A broken-down farm cart, a huge box of donkey-sized horse-shoes, a cupboard filled with sheets of gold-embossed leather, eight massive Bibles, a gigantic wooden cider press and a box of long goose quills. The list also included valuable silver and countless items of linen, a great deal of which had never been taken out of its wrapping paper.

The staff finally discovered what the inventory was for when first the silver was carted away and sold, then the linen and finally most of the other household items including much of the furniture. By this time we had been told that the Barkers were selling up and that none of the staff was to be kept on.

I confess I cried when Mrs Barker told me. They were tears of frustration rather than sorrow because I had grown to love my life as housekeeper. I had my little set of rooms just as I wanted them, I enjoyed my time off, and my system for keeping the books and staff in order was running so smoothly there was hardly a thing to do for much of the week. I was in clover and now I was to be turned out into a post-war world where people, even rich people, had less money than ever and were keeping far fewer servants than they had in the past.

To be fair to the Barkers they paid all the staff a month's wages as some recompense for the fact that we were suddenly without work, but for older servants such as Savile the prospect was more terrifying than it was even for me. If he retired he would have just the state pension and where was he to live after spending the whole of his adult life in someone else's house?

With just a few weeks to find another position I was in a panic. I remembered my mother saying that luck always favoured people who believed in good fortune so I tried to stay cheerful and look about me. Then things began to look up. The maids were found work in two big houses a few miles away. Then the gardener found something else.

A job for a housekeeper was always going to be more difficult to find but I was determined never to go back in the kitchen as either maid or cook. I vowed that if I did have to work as a maid or cook again I would apply for an assisted passage to Australia! A girl in the village had gone on a one-way ticket for just £10 and I thought it didn't sound such a bad idea if all else failed. Australia was sunny all the time and there were jobs aplenty, we heard.

But I never did have to go to Australia because in my last week with the Barkers and just a day or two before I was due to go into lodgings in Leicester and start using up my hard-earned savings there was a knock on my door and Savile came in.

He'd become a quieter, friendlier character in recent weeks. He was in truth I think a broken man. He had been there for decades and the house was his whole life. He was terrified about the future because of his age. His only option he told me was to go and live with his sister at Somers Town in London.

'I bloody hate Somers Town,' he said with a gloomy grin, 'but I've nowhere else to go.'

This was the first bit of personal information I ever got out of Savile despite all the years we had worked together. And how funny to think that we had grown up just a mile or two from each other in London, for Somers Town wasn't more than twenty minutes on the bus from Paddington.

But Savile had some great news. He explained that a big house about fifteen miles from our village might be able to offer me a job. Their housekeeper had fallen ill and been forced to retire some months ago so they needed someone straight away.

I wrote off immediately to Sir John, the owner of the hall, and received a reply just two days later inviting me to discuss the position. I put my smartest clothes on and most serious face. The postmaster in the village, Lily's father, took me in his car, which was very good of him as petrol was still rationed. I got a lift almost all the way back in a farm cart brought back into service while fuel was in short supply. This was the last time I ever travelled in a cart and I wish I had paid more attention because sitting up behind a horse was a lovely way to travel – though none of us thought anything of it until it was gone. Perhaps another reason I look back on that return journey with such pleasure is that, following my interview, I knew I'd got the job. My mother was right; I'd been optimistic and believed in luck and luck had come my way.

Chapter 43

This was to be my last house. It was a long grey-stone, three-storey building at least twice the size of the Barkers' place, but as I arrived for my inverview I noticed a number of the windows had cracked glass and there were weeds growing through the gaps in the stone terrace that ran along the front of the house. Huge windows opened on to this terrace. They must have been twelve feet high. The gravel drive was a great contrast to the house front because it was beautifully kept and during my time it was raked over every day.

Lily's father dropped me at the iron gates between their high stone pillars. The pillars were leaning and one had lost the stone ball that should have stood on top.

I felt horribly exposed as I walked along the drive. I was certain someone would come out and shout at me for trespass as this was the main entrance to the house and there might have been a separate path to the servants' door that I should have taken.

I turned right as I reached the end of the drive and walked to the side of the house and round the back where the servants' entrance was bound to be. I found it before I was discovered and pulled on a very odd-looking bell.

A little brass knob was set into a hollow place in the stone of the door surround. It was as if a circle of stone had been scooped out as a recess for the bell knob. And above the big knob in its hollow was a bold brass notice that said 'Push'. I did as I was told and pushed. Not a sound. The bell might have been a good bit off in the depths of the house which was maybe why I didn't hear it, but it was odd that when I'd pushed the knob it hadn't moved a fraction. This is no good, I thought. I tried again, pushing with all my might. It still didn't move and there was not a sound from within.

I began to feel a fool standing awkwardly at the door. At last I grabbed the brass bell pull and, ignoring the sign to push, gave it a good tug. It came out a couple of inches on a wire and a bell tinkled somewhere far away. If it was a joke to put 'Push' where it was meant to be 'Pull', I didn't think it was very funny.

Despite the post-war world of shortages and no money there were still six female staff in this house, as the mistress, Lady Emily, explained when I entered her private rooms on the first floor, having been directed there by the butler. After the Barkers, who were only middle class, I felt rather in awe of Her Ladyship as she was clearly 'out of the top drawer' as people used to say; but to give her her due she had few airs and graces and simply explained that her housekeeper had been forced to retire and she needed someone with experience to manage the affairs of the staff and the accounts.

'The number of staff is much reduced, I'm afraid,' she said, smiling apologetically as if it was all her fault and it was a poor job she was offering me. 'Do you think this would suit you despite everything?'

'I'm sure it would, Your Ladyship,' I said. 'I have been working in a similar position for a number of years. In a smaller house but managing both staff and accounts.'

'Good, excellent,' she said and then, distracted for a moment, she stared out the big window which faced down the drive. I realised that if she'd been looking twenty minutes earlier she'd have seen me traipsing uneasily towards the house in my shabby coat.

I was about to go on when she said with a smile, 'Don't worry, Mrs Clifford. We are aware of your current employment and have already received a very good reference for you by the telephone. If you are happy to start at the end of this month that would suit us admirably.'

'I'm very happy, ma'am,' I said. Her apologetic air had affected me, I realised, and I started doing the same thing. I almost felt I should apologise for accepting the position!

'Thank you. Goodbye,' she said.

And that was it. I never discovered who had spoken to her about me – I mean, which of the Barkers – but

I like to think grumpy old Savile had helped. He was a kindly man underneath it all and knew all the servants round about far better than I did because he drank with them in the local pubs.

I still had three weeks to get through after leaving the old house, which was being shut up completely, so it was just as well I'd booked my lodgings in Leicester. The landlady was quite happy for me to stay for as long as I liked with a week's notice either way, which was a relief.

But how precarious were people's lives then! Who would feel safe and secure in middle age in a dingy lodging house with little money, few possessions and not much in the way of savings?

Despite what sounds like a drab life – a lodging-house life, I mean – I was happy because I was only stuck in it for a few weeks and there were many far worse off than me. In thousands of lodging houses up and down the country were poor spinsters and retired men with no families who had just enough to pay their rent and who spent their days walking the streets and eating in cheap cafes.

When I think of all this looking back from my old age, I realise what a different world it was; a world I suspect will never come again. By the 1970s people had their own little flats, rented or bought, but back then very few had their own place and the lodging houses filled the gap, with their shabby cold bathrooms, threadbare curtains and endless bloomin' bedbugs! By the 1970s the whole world of lodging houses for the middle-aged and unmarried had disappeared.

An American man who had been unable to return home because of the war had been in the house where I lodged for some time and I met him at breakfast on the first morning after I moved in. One of the horrors of boarding houses in those days was that the residents had to eat together at the same time if they wanted their meals provided and very few landladies offered a room that didn't include food – bed and board was the norm because they made their money as much on the food as on the rooms. Meals – if they can be called meals – were provided by the landlady and served at the same time in the morning and then again in the evening.

Sam Wilson introduced himself and stood up when I reached the table. I thought, Blimey, he thinks I'm a Lady or something.

But he was just a very polite American gentleman who was I think rather lonely. We hit it off straight away and as I was no longer seeing Micky the boxer, I didn't mind being chatted up a bit – though I'm not sure Sam ever really chatted me up exactly.

Micky had vanished about a year earlier to avoid his national service, I think. He certainly wasn't a coward but I knew from my time with him that he would rather have died than go in the forces and be sent hither and thither by the system.

I told Sam that I would be moving to my new housekeeping job in a few weeks and I think he took that as a bit of a brush-off. It wasn't meant to be, so the next time I saw him I was much friendlier and we gradually drifted together. He wasn't the most exciting companion – completely different from Micky in that way – but he had a charm of his own and I found out a lot about America from him and discovered many of the byways of Leicester that I might not otherwise have found. Like most visitors he knew far more about the town than the locals.

Our short-lived relationship had a strange ending. When at last I left the lodging house to start my job Sam said he hoped he would be able to get back to America on a ship and he gave me his address in Boston and a five-pound note and asked me to write to him now and then. I wrote once or twice a year until the mid 1950s and I heard all about life in America. He eventually asked me to join him in America and marry him. Well that was one of the biggest and nicest surprises of my life, but it was too much for me to make such a move by then and I felt I hardly knew him since almost all our relationship, except those first few weeks, had been conducted by letter. But it was a romantic offer and I've wondered often since what might have happened if I'd accepted.

I sent a reply to the offer of marriage and tried to be as nice as I could but my rejection of him must have hurt because he wrote once more to say he understood and then never wrote again. I never regretted my decision because it was too late for me to start life all over again on the other side of the world. I was always too sensible for that kind of impetuous behaviour, but sometimes in an odd, quiet moment I wonder what happened in the end to poor charming Sam.

Chapter 44

I had been home to Paddington only two or three times in all the years I'd lived in Leicestershire and each time I went back I was amazed at how it had changed. The old train station was the same but all the horses had gone and also many of the houses – some demolished, others flattened by bombs during the war.

I remember going back for a few days in the early 1950s. If anything it was even blacker and more run-down than I remembered. I had returned after receiving a scrawled letter from my mother. The only part I remember was, 'Yer dad's gone off . . . Mum.'

The flat was the same as it had always been and at the top of the stairs I found the door half open and Mum sitting by the window smoking and looking out. I stood by her there and instead of the jangle and clop of horses rising from the road all I could hear was the roar of motor traffic. Mum was quite calm, even happy that Dad had disappeared, but I was amazed to hear he'd been gone more than a year before she had thought to write and tell me.

'Why didn't you write before?' I said.

'Well, he'd been going off more and more of late anyway,' she said. 'You know what he was always like. I just thought he might come back after a few weeks but when months passed I found I didn't miss him much.'

Although they didn't get on badly and certainly didn't fight much, Mum and Dad had never really seemed close. When I thought back I realised as only an adult can that they'd always lived in the same house without having much interest in each other, so what happened in the end wasn't perhaps such a surprise after all. And you know, I never heard from Dad again. I don't know if or when he died. Odd isn't it? But perhaps not as odd as people think – lots of fathers disappeared back then because it was easier to disappear. People couldn't be found if they decided to hop it. They might have a breakdown or just get bored and off they'd go. When I was a child we'd known several families where the father had lost his job or just upped and off, never to be heard of again. But how typical of my dad to leave it so late!

Mum still had her old friends to see and talk to and she had the state pension now. She hardly seemed bothered by anything any more.

'We don't care about much, do we?' she said to me later that day.

'What do you mean?' I said.

'Well, look at you. Very independent. Never married.'

And I thought, yes, she has a point. I thought I'd been too cautious ever to get married but perhaps it was just that I was too independent. But then being needy, being afraid to be on your own, always seemed a bad thing to me.

After I'd been with Mum for a few hours – and this was having not seen her for years – she suddenly said, 'I suppose you'll be wanting to get back then.'

'You're trying to get rid of me,' I joked.

'Of course I'm not. Very nice to have you back. Only I'm off to see Enid in a minute and you'd be bored.'

It was as if she wasn't there any more. I put it down to being worn out by years of bringing up children and slaving for very little return. She just wanted to be left alone, but she died a few years later without me ever seeing her again and I remember the journey up to Kensal Green Cemetery in North London where she was buried. A few of her friends were there, including Gentleman Jim, who was to play a part in my life after I retired. None of her children turned up except me and there was still no sign of Dad, but perhaps he too was dead by then.

Chapter 45

My final house was the biggest I had worked in since that very first job in Spencer House, but of course it was still nothing compared to the great houses of the past where two or three hundred servants might be under the control of the butler and housekeeper. Sir John, who would have been in his early seventies at this time, was unaware in some ways that the world had changed. He lived in the past and had the attitudes and values I think of as part of the Edwardian era.

For example he told me that I was permitted to show visitors around the house if they were 'of the right sort'. I asked the butler about that and he told me that Sir John meant only respectable people should be shown round, but he laughed and said, 'No one has come here and asked to look round in thirty years.'

This was before the days of the National Trust and hundreds of grand and not-so-grand houses suddenly open to the public. Certainly until the First World

War house visiting was something people did but it was informal – they would simply call at the gatehouse or lodge of a big house and ask if they could see round. If they looked 'the right sort' the housekeeper would conduct them through the house.

Those days were over but not it seems in Sir John's mind.

I was supposed to eat my meals with the butler and be served by the kitchen maid but in practice this rarely happened because it was a tradition that only really made sense when there were at least thirty or forty servants.

Sir John's house had been taken over by the army during the war and much of it was now in a terrible state. The damaged part of the house was closed up but I was given a tour of it shortly after I started work. The mess was awful – there was graffiti all over the walls, dust everywhere, broken windows, and most of the furniture that hadn't been broken was under filthy dust sheets.

'There's no money to sort out the mess,' said the butler ruefully.

The part of the house inhabited by the family was still impressive, however, and the Barkers' house would have fitted neatly into it a couple of times.

The housekeeper's closet – the usual small sitting room and bedroom – was at the back on the ground floor and like all country-house servants' quarters at the time it was painted a terrible sort of mental-institution green. Why they couldn't use bright colours or just white for servants in those days I don't know. Only the kitchens were ever whitewashed.

An old desk had been provided for me – it was a big double-sided thing, a partners' desk designed so each of the two partners in a business could always see what the other one was up to and make sure there was no cheating – that was how I liked to think of it, anyway!

One morning about a year after I started to use the desk for the account books and any paperwork I had to do, I pushed at a small vertical panel between two drawers and there was a click and the panel – about nine inches long and two inches wide – fell out. It was a hidden compartment stuffed full of old papers. I couldn't help having a good look at them. The earliest was dated 1790 and the most recent about 1860 so clearly the panel had been forgotten for a long time.

Some of the papers concerned rent: one said, 'Paid this Lady Day, one quarter on the Handside Paddock.' Another said, 'On account for Miss Drabble for teaching Agnes and Emily.'

And there were a few really odd ones. For example, a note written on very thick paper in a beautiful sloping hand ended with the words, 'Evening bells, Lady Kehoe, Samson, four shillings and eight pence halfpenny.'

Other bits of paper were cross-written letters. Even wealthy people sometimes did cross-writing before the Great War. A cross-written letter was written in the normal way but then turned on its side and you carried on by writing across and through the lines you had already written – at right angles to them I mean. This made letters very difficult to read if you didn't know the writer's hand really well.

If the desk hadn't been used for so long then what, I wondered, had the old housekeeper used? I never found out, but then I could discover almost nothing about my predecessor. No one would ever talk much about the old housekeeper other than to say she was a bit eccentric and bad-tempered and had been there forever. It was only after a chance remark from one of the staff – who had been sworn to secrecy – that I discovered she had been asked to retire after throwing a sharp knife at one of the maids. Usually when knives were thrown below stairs they missed their targets but unfortunately for the old housekeeper this one didn't and injured the girl.

Chubb the butler was a nice man and even older than Sir John. He'd been on the estate since he was a boy and was always lamenting how much things had changed. He loved to come to my room for a chat. I think he talked to me because all the young men who had worked in the garden and in the house before the war had refused to come back when it was over. They'd gone for other jobs with more money and more freedom. 'I'm too old to change,' he said but I think he envied the young men who had gone off to other lives.

Chapter 46

It was a sign of the times and the gradual disappearance of the old ways that I got to know Sir John far better than I had any of my previous employers. Of course strictly speaking I worked for Lady Emily, and she came down now and then to see me to discuss money issues or she would call me up to have similar conversations. But I think Sir John took a shine to me and despite his old-fashioned attitude even he had been affected by the changing world. Half a century earlier he would have addressed me – if at all – in a very formal manner, but by the late 1940s and early 1950s it was a bit embarrassing to carry on as if Queen Victoria had only just died, so people generally didn't do so. It was the Second World War that really changed everything and it always struck me as funny that all that death and destruction should have made people behave better towards each other at home.

Sir John would sometimes put his arm round me or make jokes and ask if we could have tea together in my room. So he was a strange mixture of old-fashioned and modern. I'm pretty sure he also had mental problems of some sort. He would occasionally call me Dexter or Nelly and then say, 'No, I don't think you are Dexter, are you?' He would then shake his head and carry on. He was an unusual man, very thin with pale hair brushed across his forehead and very dark eyes. He wore a close-cut full beard which made him look like Edward VII and he could go from friendly and joking to bad-tempered in a second and I think this, too, was connected to his mental problems.

He would call down two or three times a week to discuss the accounts although we never once in all the years I worked for him actually discussed them.

The first time he called for me I remember very well. He had a strange contraption he used to shout down. It was like a hollow flexible tube that ran from his study to the butler's room. He would pick up what looked like a rubber kitchen-sink plunger that was attached to a short length of hose that disappeared into the wall and bellow, 'Chubb! Chubb!', and if the butler happened not to be in his room at the other end of the hose he would just keep shouting till Chubb came back and answered or until he became exhausted or Her Ladyship told him to shut up. I think he actually preferred it if Chubb was absent because it was shouting down the tube he really enjoyed. If Chubb answered straight away His Lordship would sound disappointed and he would pretend he'd forgotten why he was calling.

Chubb very rarely shut his door if he was wandering around the servants' area and if the door was open he could always hear if Sir John wanted him.

'Oh God, he's at it again,' Chubb would say and then set off for his room. Or Cook would say, 'He hasn't bellowed much lately,' and Chubb would solemnly reply, 'No, and thank heavens for that.'

They complained about Sir John but they liked him too. I think they liked him because, like me, they remembered the sort of people we used to work for who looked at you as if they'd trodden in something!

Even when he was angry Sir John would say such funny things that it was difficult to feel you had been scolded.

I remember once I was sitting with him listening to a long description of his plans for the knot garden. He lost the thread of what he was saying and wandered over to the window for a moment. I sat patiently waiting for him to continue, knowing that this session would last about ten or fifteen minutes because it never lasted longer.

Time passed and then there was a knock on the door. Sir John went to answer it rather than simply saying 'Come in,' which is what you would have expected. I didn't hear who it was at the door but Sir John suddenly sounded very angry and he shouted, 'Well, do you want me to dance a bloody jig?' and with that he closed the door and went back to the window. After a moment he said, 'Ah yes, the garden,' and continued where he had left off telling me what he had planned.

He called me up several times to talk about the garden and it was only when he called me William once or twice that I realised he thought I was the gardener.

He did this sort of thing with Chubb too but Chubb was usually given a drink. Cook told me that Sir John very occasionally asked to see her and once he came to see her to ask if she knew who had been eating the tweezers!

But Sir John's greatest claim to eccentric fame was undoubtedly his membership of the Buckland Dining Club which met I think in Birmingham. This had started in the nineteenth century and its members ate all sorts of disgusting things just to see if they could be eaten. I think the club's origins had been relatively sane – members simply wanted to see if it was possible to extend the range of animals and birds it was possible to eat.

Sir John was an enthusiastic member and would occasionally obtain some rather odd meat which he would ask Cook to turn into a casserole or a curry. On several occasions she absolutely refused to cook the big hair-covered joints of meat that Sir John had delivered and I would step in and take over.

It was all very unorthodox but I rather liked to take a turn now and then at the kitchen stove if it kept Sir John happy; so when Cook said she just couldn't face it, I happily roasted the bit of giraffe that Sir John had obtained – God knows how – and on other occasions I cooked dormouse for him and what he told me was sea slug.

The smell of sea slug, if that's what it really was, didn't leave the kitchen for months, but Sir John and his friends loved it. Chubb said it smelled like a decaying rat which was probably about right, but once you were used to the stench released when you cleaned a grouse that's been dead for several weeks, sea slug was not much to worry about.

The Buckland dinners had originally been held at the club's premises I believe but Sir John carried them on, or at least his own version of them, at home. They were held twice a year and the motley crew who turned up were Sir John's oldest friends.

Mostly they would eat pretty normal food but with odd additions – they liked fearsomely spicy food because one old colonel had been in India where he developed a taste for it; or they would eat different species of fish caught from the local river – the sort of fish you wouldn't normally dream of eating. Cook was happy about cooking any kind of fish.

'I'll cook bloody serpents,' she said, 'just so long as they don't have fur growing on 'em!'

Old Chubb was very good at describing and even mimicking some of Sir John's friends, who, like Sir John himself, seemed a throwback to earlier times.

'They're wanting pike and eels again,' he would say, 'and the best claret, which is a terrible waste of good wine if you ask me. And I will have to put up with the usual jokes about my bloody name.'

'What do you mean?' I said.

'A chub is a kind of fish, I'm sorry to have to say, so I will have to laugh at the same old jokes again. "Hello Mr Chubb. Something rather fishy about your name. Have you been in at the deep end? You are really in the swim of it, aren't you? Do you have to carry a pike as part of your work?" And more of the same.'

Chubb seemed to be complaining but secretly I think he liked the jokes and the attention.

'They treat me like an equal in some ways,' he said. 'Except I don't get to drink the wine or even sit down.'

'Who is coming this evening?' I would ask.

'Well, there is Mr Wooley who says "Awfully good show" about twenty times in an evening, Mr North who hums the same old tune right through dinner and never says a word and old Mr Deighton who is completely deaf but shouts "What, what?" in a boom-ing voice every now and then. Honestly, I don't know how I put up with them!'

Chapter 47

A typical day at Sir John's would start at about seven thirty for me, far later and far more comfortable than those early starts I had to endure as a maid. I had my own paper delivered now at Sir John's expense and it would be brought to me by one of the maids. I would read for half an hour and then go to Chubb and see if anything special was happening that day, but really just for a gossip.

After that I'd have a look to see what was needed for the kitchen. I'd talk to Cook and she would usually give me a list for the next few days. Regular things such as milk turned up at a steady rate and the milkman left his bills which I collected and kept and noted in the accounts.

At mid-morning one of the maids would bring me a cup of coffee and I'd do a bit of knitting or read a romantic novel – what they used to call bodice-rippers, I think. Then I'd have lunch with old Chubb and in the afternoon have a walk round the house and sometimes the grounds to see if anything was amiss.

I would check that the rooms had been cleaned properly and see if we had enough cleaning materials, mops, pans and brushes, but you can imagine that it was not difficult to keep on top of all this. Once you had your system it just ticked along. I'd have tea on my own in the afternoon at about four and then dinner at six always before the family dinner at seven or eight o'clock. A pointless life you might say, living according to the rhythm of other people's lives, but I had never known anything else and we tend to stick to what we know.

I'd reached the top of the servant ladder and was more or less waited on hand and foot. I had very little to do so long as the tradesmen and staff were paid. I was into my forties now and the one thing I missed terribly was being one of the girls. The maids had to serve me and defer to me and call me Mrs Clifford so they were never going to invite me to go out dancing and I can remember the day I realised for the first time that those days were over forever.

I was a dinosaur now but truth to tell I didn't care: I felt I'd arrived somewhere. I was comfortable and able to save almost all my wages which meant I felt less worried about the future. Chubb was just as comfortable but he was far more nostalgic for the old days. He actually called them the good old days now and then and I used to tease him about it.

'Mr Chubb,' I would say in my most serious voice, 'they were not good days at all. They were awful. Don't you remember being hall boy and whacked around the head for every mistake and being paid just a few pennies a week?'

'It did me good,' he would reply. 'It's what these youngsters need.'

'But we're so much better off now, aren't we?' I would say. 'The maids treat us as if we own the house!'

'That's as may be, but there's no discipline.'

The truth is old Chubb hated having too much time on his hands because he had never learned to use time for himself. How could he when for years he had worked twelve-hour days six days a week or more?

He had only a gardener and gardener's boy to manage and it left him too much time to worry.

'Being a butler isn't just about serving wine to old fools who don't remember their own names,' he used to say. 'It's supposed to be about managing younger staff and I don't have any – well, none to speak of.'

And he was right. We both had far fewer staff than we would have had in a house of this size forty years earlier. But this was the beginning of the end, as I liked to tell Chubb. Our way of life was on the way out and it was never going to come back.

Chubb blamed motor cars and kids getting above themselves for the changes he didn't like, but money was really at the root of it.

You'd think that by the 1950s with the war being long over we'd have all had a bit more money, but somehow we didn't. We were all bumping along on the bottom. Even formerly wealthy people gradually found they had very little money.

This is why all the inhabited rooms at Sir John's house were slightly or even very shabby. He could have found the money to spruce them up a bit I'm sure but he preferred to let them fall apart rather than get by with fewer or no servants. Having to do for themselves was the ultimate indignity because servants were the upper classes' most prized possession.

The sense that things were going from bad to worse was confirmed when, one day in the early 1950s, Chubb knocked on my door. I opened it and he said, 'Sir John's asking for you.'

I went up thinking that he probably wanted to talk about money, but it was nothing of the sort. As soon as I entered the drawing room he said:

'Mrs Clifford, good of you to come up to me. Things have taken a difficult turn.'

He hummed and hawed a bit and looked out the window. Then he went very pink but still said nothing. I thought for one dreadful minute he was going to sack me on the spot or ask me to take all my clothes off!

Then he started again: 'It's a sensitive matter but my wife no longer wishes to leave the house at all. You may have noticed she has become, shall we say, a little reclusive.'

I knew what he meant because the maids and Chubb and I had commented on her increasingly strange behaviour. For at least two years she had hardly ever gone outside during daylight hours and when she did, even on hot days, she would wrap herself in a big coat and wear a scarf that half covered her face. It wasn't our place to question what was going on, but if Sir John was talking to me about it, things were clearly more serious than we had thought.

'My wife feels rather afraid of the world you see and wonders if you would mind accompanying her on a short walk each evening before she retires. I would be most grateful if you felt this was something you would be happy to do.'

Well, this was a very odd situation but I could hardly refuse.

'Where would you like me to go with Her Ladyship?' I asked.

'Just a walk round the gardens unless she asks for something else,' he replied. 'She will ring I think at about nine each evening.'

He smiled at me and turned back to his desk.

Nothing happened that evening or the next and I began to think that perhaps Her Ladyship had changed her mind or had forgotten all about it.

Then on the third day after our meeting the bell for the drawing room rang at just after nine. I didn't hear it but one of the maids knocked on my door.

'It's very odd, Mrs Clifford,' she said, 'but the drawing-room bell has rung and it never does at this time. We thought it might be a mistake.'

'Don't worry,' I said. 'I will see to it.'

I knew it must be Her Ladyship wanting to start our regular walks.

I climbed the familiar stairs at this unfamiliar hour and noticed how gloomy they looked when no light came in through the tall landing windows. I knocked on the drawing-room door and waited. No reply. I knocked again and carefully pushed the door open. Her Ladyship was sitting on the sofa by the marble fireplace looking straight at me but over a scarf that wound around her mouth and then over her head. Only her frightened eyes were visible.

I was a little frightened myself as her eyes also looked rather mad. She mumbled something while I was crossing the room. I didn't quite catch what she said so she repeated in a strange sort of guttural voice totally unlike her normal voice:

'Just quickly round the garden I think.'

She stood up and without another word made a lunge for my arm. We went down the main stairs together and I could feel her weight pulling heavily on my arm and her fingers gripping so tightly that when I checked later there were bruises on my forearm.

We went down the short flight of steps outside the main door into the dark garden and she seemed to relax. I was such an old-fashioned servant I suppose that I didn't feel I could speak freely to her. I had started work in an era when servants spoke only when they were asked a question so I thought it best to wait, but she never said a word. I could hear her breathing and there was an occasional noise like a moan. After about five minutes she said, 'Shall we go back?'

I walked her back to the house and up the gloomy steps.

In the weeks that followed this little scene was repeated perhaps two or three times a week but always after dark. Sometimes she asked to go to the rose garden, other times we took the path around the house. She very rarely spoke except to say thank you and to ask to be taken back.

Then one night things took a turn for the worse.

We had walked only twenty or thirty feet from the front door when Her Ladyship began to cry. I could hear faint sobs and gasps and then she just stopped walking and bent slightly forward, removing her arm from mine. Here was a terrible predicament. I felt sorry for her as she was clearly so distressed but the old barriers between servant and master kept me from making any gesture. But we couldn't stay there all night so I thought, Oh well, she can only sack me.

I held both her arms and pulled her towards me. I gave her a long hug of the sort you might use to comfort a child. She relaxed a little and stopped crying. Not much more than a minute passed and I thought, My you're going to get it! But no. She gently pulled away and said, 'Could we go back now, please?'

I felt I had to say something to Sir John but Chubb advised against it when I met him the next morning. The days passed and the bell stopped ringing in the evening. When I next saw Sir John to discuss the accounts he told me that his wife was in hospital where she was enjoying a break from the usual routine and a good rest.

I discovered much later that she had been diagnosed with severe depression and in those days there were no drugs to treat it. Instead she was eventually given a lobotomy, an operation to remove part of her brain in the hope that it might alleviate the symptoms.

When she returned to the house a few months after the operation it was clear that it had not been a success. Right up to the 1960s these terrible operations were almost routinely carried out on people with mental problems. Later on such barbaric treatments became illegal but it was too late for Her Ladyship and she was never right again. Within a few years she had to move permanently into a hospital where she died completely unaware of who or what she was.

With Her Ladyship gone Sir John himself gradually became more eccentric. Chubb told me that he regularly came down to the pantry just to have someone to talk to.

'He's getting funnier by the day,' said Chubb, who was genuinely saddened by the change in his master.

'The other day he said to me, "Chubb, my father thrashed me when I was a boy. Did your father thrash you?" "No sir," I said. "Clouted me more often than not but never the belt or stick." Then Sir John said, "My wife was a lesbian." And he walked out without another word. What am I supposed to make of that?'

Gradually Sir John began to refuse to throw anything away, which is a common thing in old age I think, and he used fewer and fewer rooms in the house. His supply of visitors dried up and he became a rather sad figure flitting between rooms in a dark, cold, dusty house that had once been warm and busy and full of life.

Chapter 48

The pace of change accelerated as the 1950s wore on. My job was still to look after the female staff, but we were down to one maid by 1953 so there wasn't much to do. From being rushed off my feet fourteen or fifteen hours a day I had moved to the point where I worked for about three hours a day and then put my feet up or went into the village to gossip in the post office.

The single remaining maid did the general cleaning and, Cook having left, I was now a cook-housekeeper, which may sound like a demotion but with only Sir John to look after it was a change that didn't upset me in the least. The truth is that without the cooking I would not have had enough to do – and even *with* the cooking I was often bored, and being bored in the countryside is far worse than being bored in town.

The books and accounts hardly needed looking at because our expenditure was minimal except for a handyman who insisted he would need to be paid more if he was to stop the house falling down. Sir

John was always reluctant to spend even the smallest sums on simple things such as clearing leaves from the gutters or replacing rotting window frames and broken panes, but Chubb and I would gently persuade him and it was almost as if by now we were in charge of him. True, he had to be coaxed rather than ordered about but he was like an innocent in a world he no longer understood. He had once swaggered down the steps to his waiting car giving orders and appearing in every way master of everything; now he looked rather shrunken, bashful and confused, like a king who has been deposed.

Chapter 49

I was well into my forties by now and hadn't had a boyfriend for years but I can honestly say it didn't bother me in the least because having lived alone in other people's houses so long I didn't think I could ever share my space with anyone. The truth is I was almost as stuck in the mud as Sir John, but on a trip to London I met a man who became my closest friend – although we never shared a bed or a house. He was one of those strange men who like women's company but not much more than that. I never fancied Gentleman Jim but there was something very appealing about him in a gentle, almost feminine way, and I suppose I was a bit lonely by the time I met him. Jim got his nickname from a famous American boxer who had a big pompadour haircut and was always checking to see his fingernails were clean.

Jim was actually an acquaintance of my mum. He used to call on her every now and then. I'd gone home one weekend years earlier when she was still alive. When I got to the flat she had her feet on the fender, a big coal fire going and a fag hanging out of her mouth. She must have been in her seventies by then.

'Gawd, look who it is,' she said as I came in the door. 'Put the kettle on while you're still standing.'

I found the rusty old kettle and put it on the gas.

'How's the back of beyond?' she asked. She always called anywhere outside London the back of beyond and she was certain to repeat the question several times a day. She also always endlessly repeated the same stories, but before she could get going this time, there was a knock on the door and in came a man I'd never seen before. He was a good bit younger than my mum and had a vaguely theatrical air about him.

'Oh hello,' he said glancing at me for a moment before looking back at my mum. 'Just thought you'd like some cake,' he said to her. 'I've been doing a bit of baking and I had some left over.' He put a scruffy parcel on the table and looked again at me. I was amazed at his bustling confidence and the fact that he had brought a cake. No man I'd ever met before would have gone on a visit with a cake!

'You must be Kat,' he said. 'I'd like to say your mum's always talking about you but it would be a lie. She mentioned you once, didn't you? Yes, you, you naughty old thing. What sort of a mother are you. Come on, move up.'

He sat next to me on the battered green sofa and offered me the longest cigarette I'd ever seen. For the next half hour he talked his head off in a way I wish I could recapture exactly because it was entertaining without really seeming to be and funny without making you laugh out loud.

But he almost always talked about himself.

'Well, I've spent the whole of this morning on my knees. I'm a martyr to me knees. They are bloody killing me. There must be a better way to clean the fireplace. Kat, you're in service. Rescue me. What should I do? And don't even think about telling me to get a slavey because I don't have the lolly for that.'

'You could get one of those Hoovers,' I said. 'They suck up all the dirt and you just give 'em a push and off they go.'

I'm sure Gentleman Jim knew all about Hoovers but he pretended he'd never thought of it.

'Wonderful, wonderful,' he said. 'But I bet they cost a packet. But I suppose a packet might save me a packet of woes!'

And on he went like that hardly worrying if no one ever replied. Mum stared at him as if he'd just landed from outer space but I know she liked him because she loved visitors whoever they were and many of her old cronies were dead by then. Without Gentleman Jim she'd have spent most of her last years alone.

At some stage in every conversation he would say, 'You'll never guess . . .' and then he would recount some terrific piece of gossip about someone down the road, but his gossip was never malicious.

He loved old ladies and did what he called his round, calling on the chosen few regularly to see if they needed anything. At each house he would say,

'You'll never guess. Mrs Gilbert is having her adenoids out,' or, 'You'll never guess. Old Tom's back is much worse and we all know why, don't we!'

With all the old ladies he saw each week he must have drunk hundreds of cups of tea and eaten a million biscuits, yet he was always the same slim, well-groomed, oddly picky man. The truth is that he was a genuine mystery and I never found out about him even though he played an important role in my life for many years after Mum died and I retired. I should say he was in his fifties when I first met him so only a little older than me. When he left that first time Mum looked at me and said:

'He's lived round here for a few years. Funny bugger but you sort of can't help liking him. All the old girls like him. He started coming a fair while after you left but he doesn't have any family. He's a bit of a nancy you might say, but he's been very good to me. Brings me tea and sits with me. No one else does.'

Mum was definitely losing her mind a bit by this time. I had to keep reminding her that I worked one hundred miles away. She'd frequently drop little digs into the conversation as if to say that if I cared about her I'd visit more often, 'as you're so close at hand'. She was starting to feel sorry for herself in her old age, but without Jim it would have been far worse.

As he left on that first occasion when we met at my mum's, he said, 'Come and see old Jim when you've done. She knows where I live,' and with that he nodded in Mum's direction and left.

Jim wasn't like other men in Paddington. He was always very smartly dressed and almost seemed to shine he was so clean. But if he was effeminate in some ways he could stick up for himself.

Once some kids ran after him shouting, 'Why don't you get yer hair cut, mister?'

He turned in a second and shouted at them in a venomous voice, 'Why don't you get your throats cut?'

He wasn't the only queer fish round about either. There was a woman called Bunty a few doors down from Mum who had her hair cut just like a man's and who always wore trousers and leather boots and a shirt so it was very difficult to see if she was a man or a woman. She always had a very masculine look and hardly talked to a soul, but she would lean out of her window smoking a cigarette and looking up and down the street for hours at a time. And it wasn't a good idea to catch her eye. Only Jim managed to charm her and it was odd occasionally to see Jim walking down the street with his feminine airs accompanied by big tough manly Bunty.

I didn't go to see Jim at all after that first meeting until Mum died. He was at the funeral and it was odd how he managed to distract me from the misery of the day. I was surprised at how upset I was.

We had a cup of tea and some cake back at my mum's flat afterwards and then went back to Jim's. I still thought he might make a pass at me but he didn't. I had never met a man who wasn't a real man, if you see what I mean, so it took quite a while to realise this wasn't going to happen with Jim. He showed me his collection of small metal cars and his collection of little glass figures. His flat was tiny but meticulously organised and the cleanest place I'd ever been. There were even flowers in vases, something you never saw much in Praed Street in those days.

Chapter 50

By 1955 Sir John hardly bothered to get out of bed before lunchtime and then wandered the corridors at night. He became confused and would knock on my door at all hours to ask for all sorts of strange things.

One day I heard his knock very early in the morning. We had our routine for these things now so I opened the door knowing it was him and said, 'Good morning, Sir John,' as if waking me at half past five was perfectly natural.

'Good morning, Kat,' he said. I looked expectantly at him but his mind had gone blank.

His thin hair was flattened with grease or water and the stubble stood out on his sagging jaw. It was a sad contrast to the proud figure I remembered when I first arrived at the house. He had a look of baffled absence.

I waited and then said, 'Would you like some tea, Sir John?'

'No baking then this morning?' he said.

'No, Sir John,' I replied. 'It is rather early.'

'Pity. I loved the smell you know. Cakes fresh from the oven. That sort of thing. Bread too.'

'Would you like me to bring your tea to the drawing room?'

'No, no,' he said. Then he paused. 'Do you mind terribly if I have my tea with you as I used to?'

He had never had tea with me before and I feared he mistook me for his wife or some long dead friend. He clearly no longer lived in the present and despite the differences in our lives until this moment I felt terribly sorry for him, much as, I suppose, Gentleman Jim had felt sorry for my mother. Sir John sat at the hard table and I made the tea.

For more than a year Sir John came down a few times each week very early to see me. He would then go to see Chubb and hang around the pantry saying little and clearly hating the idea of having eventually to go back upstairs to his own quarters where he would be alone.

He would potter a bit with the gardener in the afternoon and eat dinner alone served by and in the end almost spoon-fed by Chubb in that big draughty dining room.

For the last few months of 1956 I recall that Sir John would always ring for cocoa at around midnight. It was always the same. I would leave it on the table by his bed and say goodnight. He would wave and off I'd go.

And suddenly I was reminded of my last few months with old Barker at that other house years earlier. He too had asked for cocoa late in the evenings as old age and changing fortunes reduced him from a proud figure to someone who seemed to think we servants might be his friends or at least share the values he felt were disappearing.

Old people become children again and especially old people who have always had to rely on other people for the necessities of life. When the house-keeper brings the hot chocolate they are comforted and can fool themselves that things are still as they once were.

Loneliness can make us reach out to people we have hardly noticed for years.

I think I hung on as housekeeper longer than I perhaps should have because I had no idea what else to do. Slowly I began to realise that even if Sir John carried on for a few more years I could no longer stay. I had to leave and not just this job but the whole world of upstairs-downstairs.

With my mind continually on London I decided to go back where I had started all those years ago. As I turned over in my mind what to do I was amazed to find that part of my reluctance to leave came from a sense that I didn't want to abandon Sir John. On the other hand I knew that when the time came and the rest of his family intervened they would have no hesi-tation in putting me on the street.

So I gave a week's notice to Sir John and told Chubb I was off. Sir John hardly knew what it all meant but I spoke to the family lawyer when he came for his monthly visit to Sir John and he told me that he was seeking power of attorney on behalf of a cousin. He was horrified that my notice period after so many years was just one week and persuaded me to stay for another month. Chubb was cross because he felt this was the beginning of the end and that whoever took over the house would not want the old staff. He was right of course.

It probably sounds rather odd but after I left at the end of the month I never enquired what happened to Chubb and the maid. I still had the old-fashioned ideas of many in service that we were simply not meant to ask questions. And Chubb and I had never really become friends, which is not as awful as it sounds – like me he was an old-fashioned servant who kept himself to himself.

I had no real idea what I would do when I returned to London, but I felt I had to go back. My decades in the countryside were all about working and with work over, or so I thought, there was nothing to keep me there and the novelty of endless green fields had long worn off.

On the day I left I shook hands with Chubb and the maid – how formal after so many years working together! – and they looked so glum I almost felt I should change my mind and stick it out till the bitter end. But what would have been the point? The sort of housekeeper I was no longer existed. I had no desire to be the modern housekeeper who cooks and cleans and tidies up single-handed. I had no tie to anywhere except West London where it had all started so back I went to Paddington.

People say you should never go back but I felt I was going home even though home was no longer as it had been. Seeing all the changes that had taken place at least gave me something to think about. And of course there was Gentleman Jim to keep me entertained.

In the late 1950s you could find half a dozen rooms to rent in every street in London, even in Mayfair and Kensington. If you wanted a whole flat there'd be one or two in every street but they would usually be pretty horrible and you needed a great imagination to be able to see through the grime and crumbling plaster to what a flat might be.

I eventually took a flat round the corner from where I'd grown up. I spent whole days cleaning the walls and floors with carbolic and Vim until the skin fell off my fingers. In fact it got so bad I had to go to the doctor with a severe case of dermatitis – it was like being a kitchen skivvy all over again except my fingers were bleeding for *me* now.

I painted the walls myself, cleaned the cooker – which had about ten years' grease on it – and sat on the window ledges to clean the windows while the traffic roared past thirty feet below. I'd picked a top-floor flat in an old house because someone told me heat rises so it's cheaper to heat the top than the bottom because you get all the heat someone else is paying for below!

I got the flat ever so cheaply and when my trunk arrived I put my things around the place and it didn't look too bad except for the view from the back window which was into the dirtiest little yard I've ever seen. But then I'd seen a lot of dirt in my time.

Coming back to Paddington was easy in some ways but a shock in others.

I hardly knew a soul, but I remembered Gentleman Jim and after a few weeks of largely seeing no one, I thought I'd call on him. I can't say I'd been lonely in those weeks because I was so used to my own company after forty years and more alone. I just thought it would be nice to talk to someone to see if anyone Mum knew was still alive. It was only through Gentleman Jim that I had a chance of making contact with the past.

My hair, now almost entirely grey, was cut into a bob and my clothes were most definitely outdated. No one I knew as a child or youngster would have recognised me. I was just another middle-aged woman in shabby clothes shuffling to the shops. Mind you, I hadn't put on much weight and wasn't too wrinkly so I could hold my own with all the other old dears!

I knocked on Jim's door and it opened so quickly that it was almost as if he'd been standing there waiting for me. Jim was someone whose sole hobby in life was people and I reckon he was on nodding acquaintance with hundreds in Paddington in those days; but I was still so grateful when I saw a look of instant recognition in his eyes.

'Well bugger me,' he said.

Within ten minutes it was if I'd seen him every week for years instead of once in the past decade.

'Come in this minute,' he said. 'And don't even bother to suggest we have a cup of bloody tea. We're not that old yet. We're going to celebrate our heads off.'

And with that he found a bottle of gin in a cupboard and splashed it into two big glasses.

'I'll spare your blushes and add some water,' he said.

Then we sat down and had a long talk about the past.

'I'm sorry about your mum,' he said.

'Oh that was a long time ago.'

'You know she told me that she thought you'd done really well. She was always talking about how well you'd done. In fact I used to want to say "Gawd, stop going on about her, won't you," but I didn't like to. Yes, she was your fan club, so she was.'

Now I mention this little conversation because I'd always thought my mother wasn't really that bothered about any of her children. We were all so buttoned-up that she certainly never hinted at any interest in what I was doing.

When Jim said this I began to cry, something I hadn't done for years, largely I think because being in service makes you suppress all your emotions. Now

248

what little softness I still had came out just because it could and it made me think very differently about Mum. I felt sad that we'd never had a talk about how we felt when she was alive, but it was as much my fault as anyone's I suppose.

Jim was completely different from me in this respect and I learned a lot from him. He drew people to him because unlike us buttoned-up ones he was always talking about how he felt and he'd start crying at the least thing.

From then on we met every week, perhaps twice, for little outings, and he was always his same friendly interested self. I used to feel a little jealous when I had to share him with others but you know it was rather nice to have a male friend and know that there was no chance of sex making terrible complications. But though he was open about his emotions there was one closed area with Jim: he never mentioned his family.

'I like to live now,' he used to say. 'I don't like Memory Lane – too many bloody ghosts for my liking.'

And of course he was right, so when we went out we had a laugh and he took me to my first London restaurant – imagine, I was over fifty! So embarrassing, but never mind, I enjoyed it and was proud that I just about resisted the temptation to ask to see the kitchen just to make sure it was up to my standards!

When I didn't see Jim I went for walks, joined the local library and wandered the streets I'd known as a girl. Many of the poorer streets were looking even worse than they did in my childhood but here and there they were knocking the houses about dreadfully and putting up terrible concrete buildings. This process accelerated as I grew older until all I'd known had pretty much changed. I missed the old days when people really did stop and chat on the street because that happened less and less now and the population came and went far more than it had in my memory. By the 1960s whole streets were disappearing overnight, but good old Jim was always there, and then two things happened that I never would have thought possible.

I was walking down towards Portobello Road one day when I spotted a woman about my age walking towards me. I have no idea why she initially caught my attention but then as she got closer I saw the telltale strawberry birthmark. I stopped in my tracks and I'm sure my mouth fell open. I stared at her. She stared at me. She smiled and said, 'It's Kate isn't it?'

'It is,' I said, 'and you are Elsie. I can't believe it.'

I grabbed Elsie as if my life depended on it and we jumped about hugging each other in the street just as we had done half a century earlier. From then on Elsie and I were best friends again and now we had enough money for sweets and the picture palace, for tea and cakes and buns. I really did feel as if I'd come home.

Almost as good as meeting Elsie again was the fact that, a few months later, I got myself a job. And it wasn't in service.

I'd dreamed of the glamour of working in a shop when I was a girl and the most glamorous shop I knew then as now was Whiteley's, the world's first department store, in Queensway. Well, I saw an advertisement in the newspaper for a shop assistant at Whiteley's and in my best handwriting I applied for the job. And bugger me but I got it!

I loved working in the shop although I only did it for a few years. No one wore smart gloves any more and the huge rule book had vanished. I was glamorous now, no one could talk down to me and when work was over it really was over. It was as if the old world of upstairs-downstairs had never existed.

Cocoa at Midnight is part of the series
The Lives of Servants.
For a glimpse of another title in the series
read on for an extract from

The Maid's Tale,

available now.

Chapter 1

Hoxton was a rough old place in 1910 when I was born in the two rooms my mum and dad rented down a little back alley just off Hoxton Square. There were houses in the square from Elizabeth I's time with fancy doorways and windows. They were very grand houses I remember but long ago split up into cheap rooms and a bloody great family in each, but still.

Of course I didn't know any of this history at the time. I only really found out about it years after I'd left and done a bit of reading. Back then Hoxton was just where we lived and everyone would have thought you were mad if you talked about its history or the way the houses were built.

All the houses were smoke-blackened and damp. Many were propped up with timbers and we cursed the fact we had to live in them. But Hoxton was home and just the sort of poor place that thousands of girls who ended up in domestic service started from.

I had six brothers and sisters who lived and a few more born before me who died in infancy or were stillborn. My brother Jimmy died in the war. Bob went to America and died one terrible winter from the cold. A sister died from TB. But in a way we were lucky because when TB hit a family it often carried everyone off.

We did all the things that poor East Enders did. We shared beds and were boiled in summer and frozen in winter. But what always comes back to me is not the memory of those two drab little rooms we slept and ate in, but the streets and squares of the East End. That was where, as a child and a young girl, I really lived.

Chapter 2

Hoxton, Stepney and Mile End, Whitechapel and Bow. They'd all definitely seen better times. And people used to say about poor old Hoxton that it had more criminals than any other square mile in Britain. But it didn't really seem like that at the time because we were all in it together and everyone knew someone who did the odd bit of thieving. Thieving was a trade like any other, for some.

Hoxton was a bloody noisy area too. In fact it's the din that I remember most from the time I started to notice anything much round about. This would be about 1918 when the war had just ended and I was eight. It seems marvellous when I look back and think how I started in a world where horses and carts still went clattering up the streets. It was a world where I was at the bottom and seemed destined to scrub floors for my whole life. Yet I survived and lived on into a world where hardly anyone had servants. Then no one treated me like dirt just because I was what they used to call common. So didn't I travel a long way?

The hardest thing to describe about my childhood is the way East London looked and sounded and smelled. Carts were terribly noisy with their great big iron-shod wheels going over granite cobbles. Motor cars and lorries were only really just coming in. People were amazed by motors and talked about them in the way they later went on about bloody computers.

But those old motors were very noisy, too, and you can't imagine the chaos of cars and horses and carts all fighting for space with each other in the narrow roads – and the wide ones come to that – down the East End before the bombs cleared us all out.

And there were loads of other noises too. There were street vendors everywhere – well, everywhere except down the little back alleys and closes where the poorest lived and sometimes even there. All the vendors were shouting their heads off, from the cat's-meat man to dolly sellers, peg sellers and the rabbit-meat man.

Everywhere in summer there seemed to be little bands of musicians, too. There were sometimes jugglers, all sorts of street entertainers – almost always, in my memory, dark and mysterious-looking because they were nearly always foreign. I remember one little group had black hats and dark beards – we called them the Jew men. We weren't being nasty and they weren't probably Jews but what did we know? We couldn't understand a bloomin' word they said but we loved their music. They had a couple of fiddles, a squeezebox – I mean an accordion – and I think in reality they were probably Italians or gypsies.

But imagine what it was like for us who had no music at home – no radio, no TV, nothing. When you heard music out in the street you got out there as quick as you could and if you paid them a penny they might hang around and play a bit longer, and if they didn't then we'd follow them down to their next pitch.

I don't think people were so self-conscious then – us kids, girls *and* boys, would start dancing right in front of the musicians till a bit of a crowd got round us. So they'd play their violins and accordions and we'd all have a laugh. Best of all was the hurdy-gurdy man. He had a funny-looking instrument that made a lovely noise like a cross between the bagpipes and a guitar. Unless you've heard one you just can't imagine it.

Then there was the barrel organ. This wasn't played by a foreigner. It was played by an old local man and it was a two-foot-square wooden box balanced on a four-foot pole. This pole sort of leant on the old man to stop the organ toppling over. The box was polished wood with what looked like an oil painting of mountains all over one side. The old man slowly turned a handle, like a big clock key, and it played lovely tunes that made you think of a fairground. On top of the organ box there was always a sad-looking little monkey dressed in a woollen suit that tried to bite you if you got too close.

I reckon the old man had been working the streets for 50 or more years. My mother remembered him from when she was young. He had a big beard but with no moustache – you saw that a lot back then – and a pork-pie hat, waistcoat and the dirtiest trousers I've ever seen. He used to say: 'I played for the old Queen, you know.' He had a little note pinned to his organ which said he'd played for their majesties Victoria and Albert at Windsor but had fallen on hard times.

I'm sure that was a load of old rubbish but it was part of his patter. Everyone in the East End had his or her patter. Patter was a story people had ready to tell anyone who would listen – it wasn't necessarily true but it wasn't bad like a lie. It was like a sales pitch, really.

I used to worry about the organ grinder's monkey. It was small and it must have got very hot in summer, in its little suit. But no one would have thought of sticking up for the monkey, because we saw animals used for all sorts of things back then. Dogs and cats just wandered around and no one really fed them. They ate what they could find or starved – like the rest of us.

That organ grinder was a big feature of my childhood. He used to curse all the time under his breath at the poor old monkey. We thought his cursing was really funny, and sometimes we were a bit wicked and we'd tease him and run away. Then he'd get very angry and shake his fist at us, but he couldn't run after us or the organ would fall over.

The organ was one more noise that added to the great endless noise of the streets. But if it was noisy it was also bright and busy, at least in summer – it wasn't always drab like those old photos you see.

I remember the brightly painted open-top buses, rumbling in and out of the horses and carts. The buses were absolutely covered in advertisements and must have been bloody freezing in winter on account of there being no heating. We would have loved to go on them but you needed money for that – a penny a ride was too much for us.

Then, on a Sunday, it all went quiet because trading wasn't allowed then and this was enforced by the police. Sunday was a serious business even if, like us, you didn't bother with church. A lot of East Enders thought the church was a waste of time because it was another place where you were supposed to kowtow to the toffs or to God who seemed pretty posh to us. The problem was: if you didn't go to church, what did you do? The shops were shut and the pubs only opened at midday and in the evening. Most of the men waited for the pubs to open standing around on street corners talking to their mates.

The traffic, the street entertainers and the men outside pubs are among my earliest memories. Not a stick of that world is left. It might just as well have never existed. Mostly I'm glad it's gone. Apart from the poverty it was sometimes violent. People think there's too much violence in the modern world but it was much worse back then.

If any of my dad's mates had seen a man with his hair dyed red or blue like you see today they'd likely have shouted him and maybe punched him. There were a lot more street fights then, often outside pubs, and most people didn't think much of trying to stop them. They were a bit of entertainment, so they'd even egg them on. I remember as a little girl sitting outside a pub trying to get a penny for the old guy – it was November – when a fight broke out. It was half exciting and half terrifying, but it was all over in a few minutes. The two men suddenly made it up. As often as not the men who got into fights outside pubs were so drunk that they'd fight and then put their arms around each other and go back into the pub best of friends – then come out ten minutes later and start at each other again! Pubs and drink were central to our lives. Everyone drank and often from early in the morning. They'd have a nip at home and small children were still given a drop – gin I mean – to keep them quiet. People liked alcohol because they were suspicious of the water – 50 families often shared a tap and memories of typhoid outbreaks were always fresh in people's minds.

On a day-to-day level people were much harsher to each other. If there was a fight no one could phone the police because no one had a phone. Anyway people didn't trust the police. They wouldn't shout for a policeman if their lives depended on it.

It was only when a copper happened along, which was rare, that the fight would stop. I can even remember two women fighting. There they were in bright floral aprons punching and kicking each other in a street near us. I must have been about 12 years old at the time and my best friend and I were walking down a street just beyond Columbia Road market – all the houses have gone now – and we heard a right old racket going on. I looked up and saw a grey-haired woman looking out of an upstairs window and shouting at the top of her voice, 'Go on, fuckin' 'it her!'

She was leaning out of a tiny, crumbly little soot-blackened house with two storeys and one window in each storey and the front door right on the pavement. But the house was so low that even when you looked out the top window you were only about ten feet up! She was leaning out as relaxed as you like, dirty grey hair hanging down and not a tooth in her head, shouting the odds.

There was a bit of a crowd gathered and we pushed our way through to watch. These two middle-aged women were having a terrible row in front of everyone. They didn't mind a bit that people were watching and jeering because they were so furious with each other. They tore at each other's hair and scratched and kicked and I remember noticing that the men were laughing. They only butted in to pull them apart after they'd had a good long look.

You see, there was a bit of us that liked the excitement of a fight because there wasn't much entertainment. Otherwise the women did look a bit shame-faced when they were pulled apart, but then they still tried to take a swing or two at each other even after it was all over. Some of the younger children watching were crying because they were scared. But of course they'd see their older brothers and sisters laughing and soon imitate them.

What would amaze anyone now was that these wild cats were really just two old dears. Probably in their 50s or 60s, but to me, back then, they looked like a couple of grannies. And it wasn't that rare to see women fighting then. I don't remember seeing it beyond about 1940.

But for all the fights and noise and dirt our life was on the streets and not at home, which is why I remember so much from outside and so little from those two damp rooms, except the smell of small bodies in a lumpy bed and ice on the windows on winter mornings.

When you have a lot of children in one room and they hardly ever wash they smell like mice. At the time I liked the smell! It was comforting.

An invitation from the publisher

Join us at www.hodder.co.uk, or follow us
on Twitter @hodderbooks to be a part of
our community of people who love the very
best in books and reading.

Whether you want to discover more about a book
or an author, watch trailers and interviews, have the
chance to win early limited editions, or simply browse
our expert readers' selection of the very best books,
we think you'll find what you're looking for.

And if you don't, that's the place to tell us what's missing.

We love what we do, and we'd love you to be a part of it.

www.hodder.co.uk

 @hodderbooks

 HodderBooks

 HodderBooks